BLACK LOS ANGELES: THE MATURING OF THE GHETTO, 1940 - 1950

KEITH E. COLLINS

CENTURY TWENTY ONE PUBLISHING

PUBLISHED BY

**CENTURY TWENTY ONE PUBLISHING
POST OFFICE BOX 8
SARATOGA, CALIFORNIA 95070**

LIBRARY OF CONGRESS CARD CATALOG NUMBER

79-65254

I.S.B.N.

0-86548-005-2

DEDICATION

This study is dedicated to:

My Family

and

Friends

TABLE OF CONTENTS

LIST OF FIGURES

LIST OF TABLES

FOREWORD

Black Los Angeles is a unique product of black scholarship. It is the first major publication by a Black scholar, Keith Collins, and it is focused on a subject of special interest to Black people. Furthermore, its author, in the course of his research, through an imaginative application of Oral History, involved hundreds of Black Americans. The consequence of his personal commitment and the involvement of large numbers of Black witnesses is a remarkable book which all serious students of 20th century America will value.

The literature on Black Los Angeles is quite limited. Serious work is restricted to a half-dozen titles which are known to a small group of specialists. They commonly have a limited circulation and lie neglected, their existence and the insights they provide known only to a handful of serious researchers. They include J. Max Bond's unpublished dissertation, "The Negro in Los Angeles" which appeared in the mid-thirties and a very solid recent study by Larry DeGraff entitled "Negro Migration to Los Angeles, 1930-1950." The latter was also published by R & E Press. Henceforth these companion pieces will be indispensable to anyone interested in the formative years of Watts as well as the later years which saw Watts transformed into a permanent ghetto, semi-isolated by a wall of prejudice from the society of which it is a part.

BLACK LOS ANGELES focuses on a decade of mementous change and development. The Watts community emerges uncertainly in 1940, grows and stabilizes through World War II and the postwar period, its residents purposely confined to a ghetto. The thousands of people who comprise Black Los Angeles at the end of the decade find their destinies apparently fixed and predictable, barring basic structural changes in society. The urban racial ghetto of 19th century America, once thought to have been an unfortunate but necessary part of earlier Eastern society was now found to be an integral part of a modern Western America which had prided itself on boundless freedom for all individuals.

From the thousands of Watts residents, old and new, who participated in these events and developments, Keith Collins found hundreds who were especially suited to describing their lives and the times in which they lived. Each in an individual way illuminates the larger picture of which he or she was a part. And in this fashion, researcher and subject interact, cooperate, and produce an illumination of a part of the Black American past. Buttressed by material drawn from a wide range of more traditional sources, BLACK LOS ANGELES is a tribute to Keith Collins and to the hundreds of Americans, who contributed in one way or another to ensure its appearance.

David Williams
Professor of History
California State University
Long Beach, Calif. 90840

INTRODUCTION

By the end of World War I, the United States had become a nation of cities, and many of the so-called successful urban political and economic reform efforts of the late nineteenth and early twentieth century appeared to be at an end due to a lack of interest, funds, and active leadership. The largely academic and often contradicting schemes of urban sociologists, who proposed public solutions to the problems of mushrooming cities seemed strikingly out of place in the new decade of unbridled individualism. The social action programs of the progressive era were viewed as less than adequate for a nation bent on self-seeking and speculation. New buildings, new subdivisions, and new cities all reflected developers' desires rather than those of a community concerned with general welfare. What is more, a consensus seemed to grow during the 1920's that most urban problems - racial, social, political and economic would soon end automatically: the termination of European immigration would eliminate the ethnic ghetto, the dispersion of the ethnic ghetto would destroy urban bosses, the end of the urban bossism would eliminate crime and corruption, and the removal of crime and corruption would usher in a golden age for the American metropolis. The new period would be subsidized by a permanent national prosperity that would welcome the children of immigrants already here into the American middle class. However, the trickle of Black migrants into the major cities of the West and East, generally unnoticed by social and historical observers of the early twentieth century, began a trend that created an even more troublesome ghetto for the new Black arrivals who had high expectations and for the old resident whose concept of American democracy underwent a severe test.

World War II signaled the beginning of an increased and prolonged interest in city life. The war years also became a watershed for Black Americans, who began to attach the citadels of segregation and who moved to the cities in growing numbers. As urban problems and their racial components attracted America's attention, the city loomed larger and larger. Historians gradually came to share this increased interest in the city, as Allan F. Davis reported in the March 1965 issue of Social Studies.[1] The trend at the present seemed irreversible; more not less effort will be devoted to the Black history of the American city.

The literature on the Black experience in urban America is rich and voluminous. James Weldon Johnson's Black Manhattan,[2] primarily an impressionistic history of the 1920's, discussed the historical development of Blacks in New York through an analysis of the changing role of Black musicians, writers and actors.

Johnson's work has since been superseded by Gilbert Osofsky's Harlem: The Making of a Ghetto, 1890-1930. Osofsky's study of how Harlem, one of New York's most exclusive white residential areas, changed into the city's most poverty-stricken Black ghetto served as a potential model for my research in terms of migrational patterns, density, and growth. Alan Spear's Black Chicago, The Making of A Negro Ghetto, 1890-1920,[3] traced the dynamics of ghetto formation in Chicago, with emphasis upon migration, employment, and the internal leadership structure of the Black community.

Other major studies have included St. Clair Drake and Horace Clayton, Black Metropolis: A Study of Negro Life In A Northern City.[4] Their work, basically a sociological study of Black urban life, surveyed the Black community in Chicago from the early 1930's to post World War II. Kenneth Clark's Dark Ghetto: Dilemmas of Social Power[5] studied Harlem after its establishment as a ghetto, while W.E. DuBois' The Philadelphia Negro: A Social Study[6] still remains the most comprehensive sociological study of Blacks living in Philadelphia in the late nineteenth century. His methodological approach, especially oral interviews, influenced my own research.

Other recent works include Elliott M. Rudwick, Race Riot at East St. Louis, July 2, 1917,[7] and John Bracey, August Meier, Elliott Rudwick, The Rise of the Ghetto.[8] The latter, a compilation of recent scholarship, explores the process of ghetto development. Richard J. Meister, The Black Ghetto: Promised Land or Colony,[9] attempted to demonstrate the varied techniques, interpretations, and conclusions of scholars in the field.

Despite the expansion of scholarly interest in the Black urban experience, the historical literature on the rise of the Black ghetto in Los Angeles is not extensive. There are a few articles, masters' theses, and unpublished Ph.D. dissertations related to aspects of the Black experience in California, and especially Blacks in the Los Angeles area prior to the Watts' Riot of 1965. The unpublished Ph.D. dissertation of J. Max Bond, "The Negro in Los Angeles,"[10] is a sociological study, and much of it is based upon the WPA Federal Writer's Project. It is, however, a study of the Black community in Los Angeles. Professor Lawrence B. de Graaf has written the best monograph on the Black ghetto in Los Angeles: "The City of Black Angels: Emergence of the Los Angeles Ghetto, 1890-1930."[11] His work served as a model and inspiration to my own.

de Graaf established that Los Angeles already had a physically defined Black ghetto as early as the 1930's. He studied the birth and the formulative years of the area known as Watts. However, his research culminated in the late 1930's. No one has compiled a major study of Los Angeles Blacks during the critical war years 1940-1946. I propose to deal with the years 1940-1950, primarily because they provide opportunity to study the migration patterns and the impact of World War II upon the Los Angeles Black community. I propose to examine Watts and the Black community in those years in which the Black ghetto matured. I plan to extend de Graaf's work and to build upon it.

Apart from academic justification, one should point to the need to know more about the people of Watts because of what appears to be a major readjustment of politics in Los Angeles generally. This study may assist in understanding the role that Watts' residents played in the change, which culminated in the recent election of Los Angeles' first Black mayor, Thomas Bradley. In addition to Bradley, there has been a considerable growth in the number and size of city contracts let to Black businesses, an increase in Black state and federal candidates elected represent Los Angeles, and a vigorous group effort on the part of Watts' residents to influence major economic decisions in the area. In view of these changes, it is important to ask: What are the origins of Black Los Angeles generally and of its Watts residents specifically during the decade 1940-1950? This study attempts to answer these questions historically; how Watts acquired the status of a slum or a lower-class economic Black community.

I believe that World War II directly and indirectly contributed to the expansion and growth of the Los Angeles Black ghetto. Moreover, this demographic growth produced important social and political changes both within the existing Black community and between the Black community and white Los Angeles.

I intend to investigate how Watts grew during the war; what attracted Blacks to reside in the area and what type of people came, based upon interviews with approximately 450 original residents. I will also examine what happened to the original residents as the Watts area expanded in size; and finally why the area deteriorated so rapidly during the era of growth.

Watts during World War II offers the historian the opportunity to answer important questions relating to the growth of the Black ghetto in Los Angeles. Equally important, the historian must utilize both traditional methods of research and employ oral history when seeking to document and understand the life of the poor and the inarticulate who have not left traditional historical sources to be studied.

In order to answer such questions, a variety of sources were utilized, including (1) a detailed questionnaire, given to a selected sample of Watts residents who came to the area prior to but no later than 1950; (2) focused interviews obtained from influential community based politicians, church leaders, government employees, directors of funeral homes, businessmen, professionals, and "street corner philosophers" who lived in the area for some time; (3) unpublished material written by government agencies and doctoral candidates; (4) literature on housing and employment trends or patterns in Los Angeles since 1930; and (5) several court cases which were by-products of unemployment, restricted covenants, and school boundary conflicts.

Watts developed a growth pattern during the decade of 1940-1950 that could not be reversed. My study is divided into seven major parts. The first two sections provides a brief overview of Black internal migration in the United States since 1900 with considerable attention given to the years of the Great Depression and World War II. The primary concern here is with migration from Southern rural areas to Los Angeles, specifically Watts. Sections three through six analyzes the maturing of Watts into a lower-class Black community. The seventh section provides some perspective and speculation on the future condition of Blacks in Watts.

FOOTNOTES

[1] Allan F. Davis, "The American Historian vs. the City," The Social Studies, Part I, Vol. LXI, No. 3 (March, 1965), 91-96.

[2] James Weldon Johnson, Black Manhattan (1968), 126-160.

[3] Allan H. Spear, Black Chicago, The Making of a Negro Ghetto, 1890-1920 (1967), 11-91.

[4] St. Clair Drake and Horace R. Clayton, Black Metropolis: A Study of Negro Life in A Northern City, Revised and Enlarged (1962), 379-526.

[5] Kenneth B. Clark, Dark Ghetto: Dilemmas of Social Power (1965), 11-48.

[6] W.E.B. DuBois, The Philadelphia Negro: A Social Study (1967), pp. 146-259.

[7] Elliott M. Rudwick, Race Riot at East St. Louis, July 2, 1917 (1964), pp. 31-68.

[8] John Bracey, August Meier, Elliott Rudwick, The Rise of the Ghetto (1970), pp. 39-97.

[9] Richard J. Meister, The Black Ghetto: Promised Land or Colony (1972), pp. 3-63.

[10] J. Max Bond, "The Negro in Los Angeles." Unpublished Ph.D. dissertation, University of Southern California, 1936, pp. 158-199.

[11] Lawrence B. de Graaf, "Negro Migration to Los Angeles, 1930 to 1950." Unpublished Ph.D. dissertation, University of California, Los Angeles, 1962, pp. 185-252; "City of Black Angels: Emergence of the Los Angeles Ghetto, 1890-1930," The Pacific Historical Review, Volume 39, No. 3, August, 1970, pp. 323-352.

CHAPTER 1

CALIFORNIA AND THE BLACK DIASPORA

The movement of people within the borders of the United States from one city, state or region to another antedates the European colonization of North America. The participation of a substantial number of Blacks in such internal migration, however, occurred only within the last century, mainly within the last fifty years.

In California, Black migration remained very small between 1870 and 1910, but it underwent a significant change in its area of concentration. The majority of Black migrants up to 1880 settled in the gold mining areas in the Sierra Nevada Mountains, Sacramento, and San Francisco. After 1880, the completion of the Santa Fe Railroad to Los Angeles and the land boom of 1887 promoted a rapid population growth in Southern California. Los Angeles became an increasingly important destination point for Black migrants; they also remained relatively fixed in other parts of the state. By 1900, Los Angeles passed San Francisco as the leading center of Blacks in the West, but remained behind it in total population.[1] In 1910, the County of Los Angeles contained 43.4% of California's Blacks, while the city had over four times as many as any other city in the West. The total white population of Los Angeles increased at an equal rate; however, through 1910, Blacks composed only a small proportion of the city's residents.[2] Thus, California and Los Angeles were the center of Black population in the West although Blacks constituted an insignificant number in the total population. Even the earliest Black migrants met discrimination, especially in cities such as San Francisco where they were excluded from street cars during the 1870's.[3]

The majority of Black migrants were unskilled laborers, and California had an abundant supply of such workers until World War I. Chinese laborers initially entered California to work in the gold fields during the 1850's and thousands were subsequently brought in to build the Central Pacific Railroad. As the state became increasingly an agricultural area, they took over most farm labor jobs. The Federal ban on Chinese laborers in 1882 created a shortage of workers by the end of the decade, and in 1888 the California Cotton Growers and Manufacturers Association imported Southern Blacks to its farms near Bakersfield. Most of these Blacks soon migrated to urban occupations and residences. This was instrumental in discouraging further importations of Black workers and postponing the development of cotton growing in California for several decades. California's farm labor needs were adequately fulfilled by unemployed urban workers during the depression of the 1890's and then by Japanese immigrants up to World War I.[4] During the early decades of agricultural expansion in California, Blacks never gained an important position as farm laborers. No precedent was established for Black migration to rural areas in the state, and after 1910, Blacks continued to avoid these sections in spite of pleas and attractive promises from the state's agricultural interests.[5] California's Black population remained clustered in a few large urban centers, particularly Los Angeles.

The volume and importance of Black internal migration within the United States underwent a great change in the period of 1910 to 1930. During this period the mobility of Blacks equaled that of other elements of the population, and their migration out of the South became a mass exodus. Between 1910 and 1920, the estimated net migration of Blacks from the South was 454,000; during the 1920's, it was 749,000.[6] Table I on the next page is quite helpful in providing a capsule summary of the growing numbers of five minority groups in the state of California between 1900 and 1960. The out-migration in both decades far exceeded that of any previous ones and caused a significant geographical redistribution of the American Black population. Containing 89 percent of it in 1910, the South had only 78.7 percent by 1930.[7] Unlike earlier decades, a significant number of Blacks left states in the lower South. The greatest out-migration during the first decade came from Mississippi, South Carolina, Georgia, and Alabama. In the 1920's, the largest net loss was borne by the South Atlantic States, especially Georgia and South Carolina.[8] Where earlier migrations had contained few Blacks in the lowest economic brackets and from rural areas, the movement after 1915 attracted a large number of unskilled urban workers and farmers.

Several thousand Blacks had been imported to mining areas of the Rocky Mountain States when the Mexican Revolution and World War I reduced the sources of cheap labor, but this area of employment declined greatly in the 1920's. The lack of industry and the depressed condition of wheat and corn farming left no other fields of employment to Blacks released from mining jobs, and the Mountain States suffered a net out-migration and a decline of 576 in the Black population from 1920-1930. Washington and Oregon likewise had almost no increase in their small Black population.[9]

In contrast to these other Western States, California received a significant Black in-migration during the decades 1910-1930. The net in-migration of Blacks between 1910 and 1920 has been estimated at 16,100. In the following decade it reached 36,400, while the rest of the region experienced a net out-migration. The proportion of the West's Blacks living in California rose from 43 percent in 1910 to over 66 percent by 1930, and California became the logical center of subsequent migrations of Blacks to the West.[10] A majority of Blacks entering California during these decades showed an equally significant tendency to concentrate in the Los Angeles area. Very few moved to rural sections, and by 1930 less than 3,000 were employed in agriculture, mainly as wage laborers.[11] Other cities in the state also received few Blacks and fell steadily behind Los Angeles whose Black population increased 31,295, or 41.2 percent between 1910 and 1930. Containing 35.6 percent of the state's Blacks in 1910, Los Angeles had 48 percent by 1930, and the county contained over 57 percent.[12]

6

TABLE I

POPULATION BY RACE, CALIFORNIA – 1900–1960

Race	1900	1910	1920	1930	1940	1950	1960
Total	1,485,053	2,377,549	3,426,861	5,677,251	6,907,387	10,586,223	15,717,204
White	1,402,727	2,259,672	3,264,711	5,408,260	6,596,763	9,915,173	14,455,230
Nonwhite	82,326	117,877	162,150	268,991	310,624	671,050	1,261,974
Negro	11,045	21,645	38,763	81,048	124,306	462,172	883,861
Percent of Total	0.7	0.9	1.1	1.4	1.8	4.4	5.6
Percent of Nonwhite	13.4	18.4	23.9	30.1	40.0	68.9	70.0
Indian	15,377	16,371	17,360	19,212	18,675	19,947	39,014
Japanese	10,151	41,356	71,952	97,456	93,717	84,956	157,317
Chinese	45,753	36,248	28,812	37,361	39,556	58,324	95,600
Filipino	--	5	2,674	30,470	31,408	40,424	65,459
All Other	--	2,252	2,589	3,444	2,962	5,227	20,723

SOURCE: Negro Californians: "Population, Employment, Income, and Education," State of California Department of Industrial Relations (San Francisco, California, June 1963), pp. 9-11.

7

During the period 1910 to 1930, Blacks remained an insignificant minority of the migrants and total population in the West, but their migration became increasingly concentrated in one city of that region, whose Black population by 1930 approached that of some Eastern and Midwestern terminal of the "Great Migration."

Extensive migration to California and declining movement to other Western states were not, of course, unique characteristics of Black migration; they were an outstanding feature of total population movement between 1910 and 1930. California had the largest net in-migration of any state in both decades, estimated at 804,100 in the first and 1,695,200 in the second.[13] A large majority of the new migrants settled in urban areas, with Los Angeles the prime area of concentration. Its total population rose from 319,198 in 1910 to 1,238,048 in 1930, passing San Francisco in 1920 and nearly doubling that city's population by 1930. In general, Black migrants to the West followed the direction of movement of the total population.[14] This more complete statistical explanation of Black migration is depicted for three decades in Table II on the next page.

Similarly, the factors which lured whites to California also attracted Black migrants. Extensive advertising of California's climate by writers, businessmen, and private groups such as the All-Year Club of Southern California or the California Boosters' Club brought many persons to the state for vacations and often for permanent residence. Real estate promoters also found the climate a strong argument for attracting potential customers:[15]

Nowhere else probably are (realtors)...so successful
in selling sunshine and bungalows, bare lots and
sunshine, mountains and sunshine or just plain sunshine itself. The "sunshine", that's California's
stock in trade...[16]

The California Realty Board, headed by Sydney P. Doaner, during the 1920's, became one of the most active advertisers attempting to lure Blacks to Los Angeles.

The boom in new industries and the general prosperity of California between 1910 and 1930 also attracted migrants. The motion picture of oil industries underwent tremendous growth which provided jobs for several thousand persons and created an image of prosperity. The increase of population and tourist traffic created many service jobs which assured many migrants of employment up to 1929. Blacks, excluded from the oil industry and the movie studios, nonetheless found employment in service jobs, particularly domestic work and transportation. The home construction boom of the early 1920's became another important area of Black employment.[17] More attractive to migrants than the jobs themselves were the wages offered by California employers. Black artisans in the mid-1920's, for example, earned up to $14.00 a day and unskilled workers received up to $5.00 for eight hours work.[18] Such wage scales were among the highest in the nation.

TABLE II

NEGRO POPULATIONS OF U.S., WEST, CALIFORNIA, AND LOS ANGELES
AND PROPORTION TO TOTAL POPULATIONS, 1910-1930

Area	1910	1920	1930
Negro Population			
United States	9,827,763	10,463,131	11,891,143
West	50,662	78,591	120,347
California	21,645	38,763	81,048
Los Angeles County	9,424	18,738	46,425
Los Angeles	7,599	15,579	38,894
Percent of Population Negro			
United States	10.7	9.9	9.7
West	0.7	0.9	1.0
California	0.9	1.1	1.4
Los Angeles County	1.9	2.0	2.1
Los Angeles	2.4	2.7	3.1

Negroes in the U.S., 1920-32, pp. 5, 9, 13, 15, 55; Negro Population, 11890-1915, pp. 767, 800; Fifteenth Census, Population, III,
Part I, p. 252; U.S. Bureau of the Census, Fourteenth Census of the
United States...1920, Vol. III, Population, Composition and Characteristics of the Population (Washington, D.C., 1922), p. 114.

While Los Angeles had many appealing characteristics, the migration of Blacks to that city did not receive the same organized support
provided by Northern cities. Letters from friends and relatives encouraged many Blacks to come to Los Angeles, but its main Black journal,
the California Eagle, remained aloof from efforts to lure out-of-state
residents. The Eagle frequently criticized the condition of Blacks
in Los Angeles and a few articles discouraged movement to the city.[19]
This attitude contrasted sharply with the intensive promotion of the
"Great Migration" by Northern Black journals. Popular magazines,
private booster clubs, and real estate advertisers concentrated their
promotion of California on whites, and the absence of a widely distri-
buted Black paper left many unaware of the promises of Southern
California. The fact that Los Angeles industries did not during this
era send labor agents into the South also left California under-
promoted.

Many Blacks, attracted to Los Angeles between 1910 and 1930,
found that the streets were not paved with gold. Black housing became

increasingly restricted and isolated in the central portion of the
city, shaped in part by the erection of a Central Avenue hotel in 1912
which catered to Black tenants. Many white property owners in this
area sold or rented to Blacks and the Central Avenue district became
their main area of residence.[20] They also moved into Watts, Eastern
Los Angeles, and the West Adams district during the 1920's. After
1918, white property owners and realtors became increasingly hostile
to Blacks moving into all-white neighborhoods, and new migrants settled in sections already occupied by Blacks.

Housing restrictions, encouraged by court cases enforcing racial
covenants which prevented the "use of occupancy of property by Blacks,"
spread throughout Los Angeles and gained support from several suburban
newspapers, many realtors, and the Ku Klux Klan.[21] By 1930, 70 percent
of Los Angeles' Blacks lived in one Assembly District in the Central
Avenue area. The remainder lived in adjacent sections. Many of these
houses had only two to six rooms, lacked sanitary facilities, and were
maintained in a dirty, unrepaired condition.[22]

Personal disrespect combined with legal discrimination continued
to be the cominant white mood toward Blacks during the 1910 to 1930
period, and the Black migrant found manifestations of this mood in
Los Angeles. Restaurants outside the "colored" district refused to
serve them, hotels would not lodge them, and they were excluded from
many theaters. Racial discrimination provided little protest from
state or local governments. In 1922 a woman who sued a restaurant
owner for refusing service was coldly told by the judge that she had
no business patronizing white restaurants.[23] Many public accommodations remained partly or entirely closed to Blacks, especially in
suburban cities around Los Angeles. Residents of several coastal
towns prohibited Blacks from visiting their beaches or erecting bath
houses on them, even in cases where Blacks owned the beach property
involved. The city of Pasadena excluded them from most of its public
parks, and in 1918 set up an exclusive Black playground to avoid
admitting colored children to others.[24] Such behavior was greatly
strengthened by the rise of a substantial Ku Klux Klan organization
in Southern California during the early 1920's.

The most vivid expression of Los Angeles' discriminatory mood
toward Blacks was the popularity of the jitney buses - privately
operated buses unregulated by the city - during the years after 1910.
These buses refused to accept Black passengers and ejected those who
managed to get aboard. Jitney operators appealed to Jim Crow sentiments as one reason why the voters should not regulate them:

To Our Jitney Patrons:
    Why should you vote for the jitney?...Because
your wife and daughter are not compelled to stand
up while negro (sic) men and women sit down. If
you vote yes on No. 4 you will put us out of
business.[25]

Blacks were also dissuaded from moving to the Los Angeles area by geographic and economic factors. The trip from most Southern states, long and costly, discouraged migration to California during the 1920's by automobile due to the very poor roads throughout much of the Western United States. A migrant coming from Arkansas in 1922 reported finding no paved road from northwestern Arkansas through Oklahoma, New Mexico, Arizona, and eastern California until he reached Cajon Pass. Even when paved roads were installed at the end of the decade, they remained very narrow and rough.[26] Families who chose to move by train had to pay for the transport of any freight they chose to bring with them and passenger fares remained considerably higher than those to most Northern cities due to the greater distance. Southern Blacks did not have the precedent for migrating to the West that they had elsewhere, since few had relatives or friends in California.

Economic opportunities, the greatest motive for internal migration, remained limited for Blacks in Los Angeles when compared to Northern cities. Industrial jobs were especially small in number. In 1909, Los Angeles, relatively insignificant as an industrial center, ranked fortieth among American cities in the number of wage earners employed. While it rose rapidly in the next two decades, it still remained less industrialized and offered only half as many jobs as most Northern centers of Black in-migration. In 1919, it ranked nineteenth in the number of wage earners; by 1929, it was still only thirteenth.[27] Furthermore, Blacks could obtain only a small proportion of the industrial jobs available.

The presence of a white labor force adequate for the industries of the Los Angeles area gave management little reason to hire Blacks and some excuse for not doing so. Most manufacturers took the attitude that Black and white workers "didn't mix" and perpetuated the exclusion of Blacks from many jobs. A survey of 456 Los Angeles industries in 1926 found only 50 which employed whites and Blacks together, and in 1930 Black workers composed only 2.1 percent of the males engaged in manufacturing. The number of Blacks working as artisans declined during the 1920's, and they obtained little employment in clerical or white collar jobs.[28] A few Black business firms prospered, most notably the Golden State Life Insurance Company, but the Black community on the whole lacked the capital to establish a significant number of enterprises. Black business initiative was also hampered by a lack of entrepreneurial experience and the reluctance of Blacks to patronize their own stores.[29]

The absence of employment opportunities for Blacks in the Los Angeles area was dramatized by the fact that some of the most widely promoted business plans attempted to attract the Black population to sparsely-settled farm lands. During World War I and the early 1920's the California Eagle repeatedly urged Blacks to leave the city and build themselves a more prosperous future in California agriculture. The few articles it published encouraging Blacks to migrate to California emphasized the opportunities of farm ownership.[30] A typical editorial urged:

...it's up to all the forces that really stand for
race advancement to encourage the movement "back
to the soil." There are yet yawning opportunities
in the Imperial Valley, on the Salton Sea, as well
as in the Paul (Palo) Verde Valley, and some of
our very representative citizens are presenting
marvelous opportunities in Lower California... The
sad, sickening spectacle of herding up in the cities,
living from hand to mouth, is a reflection when a
competence and contentment is so near at hand.[31]

A group of Blacks accepted this call during World War I and organized
a land development company which purchased tracts in Baja California
and urged Blacks in Los Angeles to buy stock in the company. Despite
vigorous promotion, few Blacks supported the company, and it disappeared
during the 1920's.[32] No "back to the soil" movement developed among
Blacks residing in or moving to Los Angeles between 1910 and 1930, and
the Black farm population in California remained a small fraction of
the growing number in urban areas. Most Blacks preferred to accept
even menial city jobs as domestic servants, service workers, truck
drivers, mechanics, and common laborers.[33]

When seeking unskilled occupations, Blacks met heavy competition
from another avenue of migration. Foreign immigration to California
fulfilled much of the need for unskilled laborers and restricted the
demand for Black migrants to perform such jobs. While European immigration to other regions of the United States fell tremendously after
1914, the number of foreigners entering California mounted. Japanese
immigration continued until the Exclusion Act of 1924. Moreover, the
number of Mexican nationals entering California and Los Angeles increased during World War I and grew at a rapid rate throughout the
1920's since the restricted immigration laws did not apply to them.
By 1930 there were 368,013 Mexicans in the state and 97,116 in the
city of Los Angeles. After 1920, there followed a substantial influx
of Filipinos.[34] This immigration, Oriental and Mexican combined,
greatly outnumbered Blacks in California and Los Angeles up to 1930.
Table III immediately following further substantiates the conclusions
reached here.

The majority of Orientals and Mexicans found employment as laborers, limiting the employment opportunities for Blacks in that type
of work. Mexicans and Filipinos supplied nearly all the labor needed
by California agriculture.[35] Minority groups and European immigrants
provided serious competition in unskilled industrial jobs and in
service occupations, especially during World War I.

Just before 1918 foreign immigration of both Nordics
and Japanese seemed to push the Negro from all industrial lines of work, and threatened his status in the
domestic field. Even the seemingly inapproachable
shoe-shining field was competed for by the Greeks.

12

Trained English servants succeeded them as valets
and butlers. Mexican labor had ever since 1910
been a serious bone of contention for the unskilled
Negro laborer. Influx of Negro migrants from the
South after 1918, caused a serious employment situation, because the majority were without a trade and
could not enter into the slowly ascending Negro
industrial center.[36]

TABLE III

NEGRO AND OTHER MINORITY RACE POPULATIONS OF
CALIFORNIA AND LOS ANGELES, 1910-30

| Area & Race | Population | | | Percentage of Total Population | | |
	1910	1920	1930	1910	1920	1930
California						
Negro	21,645	38,763	81,048	0.9	1.1	1.4
Other Races	144,623	244,563	555,956	6.1	7.1	9.8
Los Angeles						
Negro	7,599	15,579	38,894	2.4	2.7	3.1
Other Races	6,292[a]	43,987	125,570	2.0	7.6	10.1

[a] Census figures in Los Angeles for 1910 count only Orientals
and Indians; no figures were available for Mexicans. Statistics for
California in 1910, and all figures for 1920 and 1930, include Mexicans
with Other Races.

Fifteenth Census, Population, II, pp. 52, 69.

An expansion of unskilled jobs in California after 1922 lessened the
employment crisis, but the immigrant population remained an obstacle
to Blacks who sought unskilled jobs throughout the 1920's. This and
other deterrents did not prevent a substantial number of Blacks from
moving to Los Angeles, but they did limit their migration during the
period.

A survey of Black migration to the West up to 1930 must conclude
that Blacks were most conspicuous in the region by their absence.
Largely unsettled prior to the Civil War, the West received only a
handful of slaves, and the immobility of the Black population up to
1910 kept the majority in the South. In the following decades Blacks

13

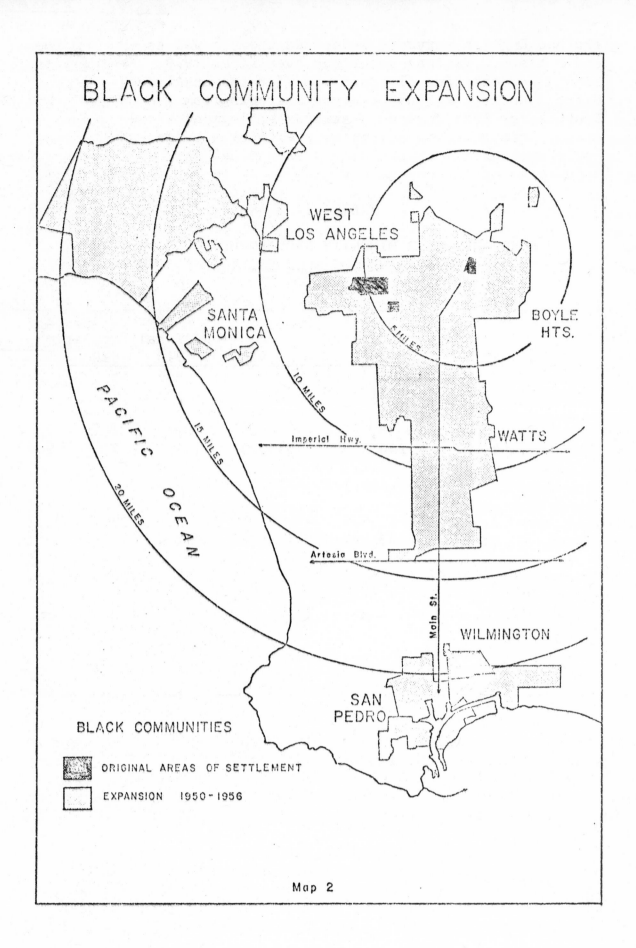

BLACK COMMUNITY EXPANSION

WEST
LOS ANGELES

SANTA
MONICA

BOYLE
HTS.

PACIFIC OCEAN

5 MILES

10 MILES

15 MILES

20 MILES

Imperial Hwy.

WATTS

Artesia Blvd.

Main St.

WILMINGTON

SAN
PEDRO

BLACK COMMUNITIES

ORIGINAL AREAS OF SETTLEMENT

EXPANSION 1950-1956

Map 2

14

became more mobile, and between 1915 and 1929, many joined the "Great Migration" from the South to Northern cities east of the Mississippi. But the number of Blacks moving to the West remained insignificant with one conspicuous exception - Los Angeles. The map on the previous page provides an illustration of the early settlement and subsequent expansion of the Black community in the Los Angeles area. However, even the growth of the Black community remained obscured by the general white migration to California and the comparative absence of Blacks from the region as a whole. Not until the nation had gone through a decade of depression did larger numbers of Blacks break their tradi- tional attachment to the South and begin a mass movement to the West.

FOOTNOTES

[1] U.S. Census Office, Population of the United States at the Eleventh Census: 1890, Part I (Washington, 1895), pp. 451-452; U.S. Census Office, Twelfth Census of the United States...1900, Vol. 1, Population, Part I (Washington, 1901), pp. 76,78; U.S. Bureau of the Census, Fourteenth Census of the United States...1920, Vol. II, Population, General Report (Washington, 1922), pp. 52-58.

[2] U.S. Bureau of the Census. The Fifteenth Census of the United States: (Washington, 1918), pp. 43, 51; Negro Population, 1890-1915. Government Printing Office.

[3] Deliliah Beaseley, Negro Trail Blazers to California (Los Angeles, 1919), pp. 37, 54-62, 65.

[4] U.S. Congress, Senate, Subcommittee of Committee on Education and Labor, Hearings, Violations of Free Speech and Rights of Labor, 76th Congress, 3rd Session, Part 47, 1939, pp. 17313-14. Hereafter cited as Senate Committee on Education and Labor, Hearings, La Follette Subcommittee, Part 47.

[5] Lawrence Brooks de Graaf, "Negro Migration to Los Angeles, 1930 to 1950" (unpublished Ph.D. dissertation, Department of History, Univer- sity of California at Los Angeles, 1962), pp. 17-19.

[6] Everett S. Lee, et al. Population Redistribution and Economic Growth, United States 1870-1950 (1957), pp. 4-11.

[7] Sterling D. Spero and Abram L. Harris, The Black Worker: The Negro and the Labor Movement (1931), pp. 32-33.

[8] Ibid., pp. 9, 12; Lee, et al, loc. cit.

[9] Lee, et al, loc. cit.; Population Redistribution and Economic Growth, I, Table P-1; Negroes in the U.S., 1920-1932, p. 9.

[10] Lee, et al, *loc. cit.*; *Negroes in the U.S., 1920-1932*, pp. 5, 9, 13, 15.

[11] U.S. Bureau of the Census, *Fifteenth Census of the United States: 1930, Population*, Vol. IV, Occupations (1933), p. 193. Hereafter cited as *Fifteenth Census, Population IV*.

[12] *Negroes in the U.S., 1920-1932*, pp. 55, 66; U.S. Bureau of Census, *Fifteenth Census of the United States: 1930, Population*, Vol. III, Composition and Characteristics of the Population, Part I (1932), p. 252.

[13] Lee, *et al, loc. cit.*

[14] John Kieran (ed.), *Information Please Almanac, 1951* (1950), pp. 77, 79, 80, 89.

[15] Carey McWilliams, *Southern California Country* (1946), pp. 135-137. This widespread advertising subsequently proved to be embarrassing, for the bright picture it painted of Southern California continued to attract many Black migrants when employment opportunities were scarce.

[16] *California Eagle*, December 26, 1924, p. 1.

[17] "Summary Report of White Collar and Skilled Negro Survey, Los Angeles County, 1935-36," prepared by the Works Progress Administration (Los Angeles, n.d.), pp. 18-38. Hereafter cited as "White Collar and Skilled Negro Survey, Los Angeles."

[18] *California Eagle*, June 9, 1933, p. 12.

[19] This analysis is based on a study of issues of the *California Eagle* from 1916 to 1929. Other Black journals were set up from time to time, but the *Eagle*, which was started in 1892, was the only paper which remained solvent over a long period, and it had the widest circulation of any Negro journal in California. While the *Eagle* did not encourage Blacks to move to Los Angeles, it did urge them to migrate to California farm lands, June 9, 1933, pp. 38-39.

[20] "The story of the Negro in Los Angeles County," prepared by the Works Progress Administration, Federal Writers' Project (N.P., 1936), pp. 6-7. Hereafter cited as "Negro in Los Angeles County."

[21] *Ibid.*: "Negro in Los Angeles County," pp. 46-47. *California Eagle*, April 4, 1924, p. 1; May 9, 1924, p. 14.

[22] "Negro in Los Angeles County," pp. 49-50.

[23] *California Eagle*, November 25, 1922, p. 1; October 1, 1921, p. 8.

[24] Ibid., June 3, 1922, p. 1; July 4, 1924, p. 1; Anniversary Edition, September, 1919, p. 10.

[25] Ibid., June 2, 1917, p. 1. The 1917 election resulted in the city regulation of jitneys, but according to Professor de Graaf there is no evidence that the buses were immediately put out of business or compelled to end their jim Crow practices. However, the California Eagle carried no articles complaining of discrimination of jitneys after 1917.

[26] Lawrence Brooks de Graaf, "Negro Migration to Los Angeles, 1930 to 1950," unpublished Ph.D. dissertation, Department of History, University of California at Los Angeles (1962), pp. 35-38.

[27] U.S. Bureau of the Census, Thirteenth Census of the United States... 1910, Vol. VIII, Manufacturers 1909, General Report (Washington, 1913), p. 84; U.S. Bureau of the Census, Fourteenth Census of the United States...1920, Vol. VIII, Manufacturers 1919, General Report (Washington, 1923), p. 19; U.S. Bureau of the Census, Fifteenth Census of the United States: 1930, Manufacturers 1929, Vol. 1, General Report (Washington, 1933), p. 243.

[28] "Negro in Los Angeles County," pp. 51-53.

[29] California Eagle, June 30, 1933, p. 3.

[30] Ibid., February 9, 1918, p. 1.

[31] Ibid., January 17, 1918, p. 1.

[32] Lawrence Brooks de Graaf, "Negro Migration to Los Angeles, 1930-1950," unpublished Ph.D. dissertation, Department of History, University of California at Los Angeles (1962), pp. 110-112.

[33] U.S. Bureau of the Census, Fifteenth Census of the United States: 1930, Population, Vol. IV, Occupations (Washington, 1933), p. 193. Hereafter cited as Fifteenth Census, Population, IV, pp. 199-202.

[34] U.S. Congress, Senate, Subcommittee on Education and Labor, Hearings, Violations of Free Speech and Rights of Labor, 76th Congress, 3rd Session, Part 47, 1939, pp. 17313-14. Hereafter cited as Senate Committee on Education and Labor, Hearings, La Follette Subcommittee, Part 47.

[35] Senate Committee on Education and Labor, Hearings, La Follette Subcommittee, Part 47, p. 17315.

[36] "Negro in Los Angeles County," pp. 50-51.

CHAPTER 2

DEPRESSION, WAR, AND CALIFORNIA'S BLACK MIGRANTS

The majority of Blacks who came to California normally settled in a few metropolitan areas. By 1950, in fact, they were concentrated in cities more than in any previous decade. The proportion of California's Black population in metropolitan areas increased 87.6 percent to 90.5 percent.[1] Most of this increase took place during World War II when thousands of Blacks streamed to western war production centers. The largest number went to Los Angeles, but they also moved to several other cities on the Pacific Coast which had not attracted them before. The wartime movement to San Diego, Portland, Oregon and Seattle, Washington swelled their Black communities tow and three fold, respectively; in the postwar period the Bakersfield area also received a considerable net in-migration.[2] The most phenomenal increase occurred in the San Francisco-Oakland metropolitan area. In the last year of the war the Bay area attracted many Blacks from Los Angeles as well as other states at an accelerated rate which reached its peak in January, 1945. The number of San Francisco Blacks nearly doubled between April, 1944 and August, 1945; in Alameda it increased by 26.77 percent between April, 1944 and August, 1945; in Richmond it grew 50.04 percent up to September, 1947.[3] The postwar period saw a marked decline in the rate of growth of Bay area Black communities, and some cities had small out-migrations of Blacks. However, approximately 85 percent of the wartime migrants remained. The San Francisco-Oakland area had a decennial increase of approximately 125,000 Blacks, nearly as large as Los Angeles, and the two metropolises contained over 79 percent of the state's Black population.

The substantial movement of Blacks to other cities within California did not alter the position of Los Angeles as their chief destination and center of residence. It became the focal point of their migration during most of World War II. Between 1940 and 1950 the number of Blacks in the city increased 107,435. They composed a much larger proportion of the migrants coming to Los Angeles than in previous periods as well as an increasing percentage of its total residents. The first large influx came in the Spring of 1942 when the Southern Pacific Railroad Company imported workers from Southern states. During the peak of this operation, Blacks entered Los Angeles at a rate of 300 to 400 per day; the entire importation brought close to 3,100. Few of the people imported obtained permanent jobs, as the railroad quickly abandoned its policy of enlisting Southern Blacks in favor of hiring Mexican nationals. However, most of these workers remained in Los Angeles, and their letters to relatives and friends in other states attracted additional waves of Blacks.[4]

Once begun, the mass migration of Blacks to Los Angeles mounted rapidly. It reached its peak in June, 1943 when between 10,200 and

12,000 Blacks entered the city. The number arriving in July and
August were as large. Considering that the net in-migration averaged
approximately 15,000 per month during this period and that attractive
working conditions and the availability of jobs induced a majority of
the Blacks who came to Los Angeles to remain there, they may have composed as much as 50 percent of Los Angeles' immigrants in the summer
of 1943.

Blacks continued to move to Los Angeles after 1943, but their
numbers declined sharply in the last year of the war. Between April,
1944 and January, 1946 the Black population increased by only 14,194.
This was the lowest annual rate of growth of any of the three intervals
between censuses during the decade.[5] During the last four years of the
decade, the Black population grew at a faster rate, rising 38,127. No
figures are available on the proportion of migrants and natural increase
in this figure, but many Blacks continued to enter the city. During
the recession of 1949 the number of non-whites moving to Los Angeles
metropolitan area declined to 9,225, of whom over 6,300 were from other
states. They composed only 4.7 percent of the total increase; however,
their net in-migration of 1,780 constituted 15.3 percent of the total.[6]

The volume of Black migration to Los Angeles varied greatly from
that to other urban areas in California during the 1940's. In the
first four years of the decade, Los Angeles continued to attract a
majority of the Blacks moving to California, as it had during the 1920's
and 1930's. Its Black population growth exceeded that of all the other
large cities in the state. After 1943, fewer Blacks settled in Los
Angeles, while many moved to other cities. Their settlement in San
Francisco increased more than in Los Angeles between 1944 and 1946,
and several other cities developed Black communities that attracted a
large number of the migrants. In the second half of the decade, Los
Angeles regained its status as the leading destination of Blacks moving
to California. Their population in that city increased more than one
and one-half as much as that of San Francisco, Oakland, or San Diego.
In 1949 the Los Angeles metropolitan area received over one-half of
the net immigration of non-whites to California while neither San Diego
nor San Francisco-Oakland had any appreciable gain.[7]

Blacks moving to the Los Angeles area during World War II tended
to settle in the established Black community in the central city, while
only a small number inhabited the rapidly expanding suburbs. By 1950,
Los Angeles city contained 78 percent of the Blacks in the county, as
compared with 47 percent of the total population. A few cities bor-
dering Los Angeles with substantial Black populations in 1940 continued
to attract them, above all Pasadena which contained 7,820 by 1950.
Long Beach had the most outstanding growth, from 610 in 1940 to 4,267
by the end of the decade. Santa Monica, Compton, and Monrovia were
the only other cities with over 1,000 Black inhabitants in 1950.[8]
Many suburban communities which grew from vacant fields to cities
during the 1940's often contained only five or ten Blacks throughout
the decade. Housing segregation kept most of them closely confined
to pre-war areas of settlement. Their community in Los Angeles city,

already overcrowded by 1940, expanded very little and housing congestion became one of its most serious problems.

Internal migration during the 1940's made Blacks a significant element in Los Angeles, as well as in several other cities of the Pacific Coast, and altered the pattern of their movements within the nation. While the volume of their movement fluctuated during the decade, the trend of the Black influx to Los Angeles is never reversed or halted. Black in-migrants exceeded those who left the city throughout the decade, and they formed a steadily rising proportion of its population. In 1940, they accounted for 6.5 percent of its inhabitants; by 1950, Blacks composed 10.7 percent. The tremendous influx maintained Los Angeles as the largest Black community in the West, in spite of the substantial growth of others in the San Francisco Bay area, and made it number eight in the nation.[9] The evolution of a large movement of Blacks to the Pacific Coast had been forecast by their small influxes to Los Angeles during the 1920's and 1930's and by the leading position of California in interstate population movements in both decades. However, it is not until the entry of the United States into the Second World War that conditions in Los Angeles and California, compared with those in other areas, attracted a mass migration for Blacks.

The tremendous growth of California's industrial plants during World War II spurred the Black migration. In 1939 California provided only 3.5 percent of the nation's jobs in industry. The Roosevelt Administration's program of military production led to a great expansion of industrial facilities in Los Angeles, San Diego, San Francisco, and Oakland. The concentration of aircraft factories in Southern California, the proximity of the state to the Pacific theater, and a climate suited to year-round production, testing, and troop training expanded government contracts for military goods and facilities. Wage and salary workers in Southern California rose from 1,812,000 in 1939 to 3,084,000 in 1943, a gain of 70.2 percent, nearly double the rate for the nation. In Los Angeles County employment grew from approximately 900,000 in March, 1940 to 1,450,000 by October, 1943, an increase of over 60 percent. Los Angeles aircraft plants employed the largest number, followed by the shipyards. By 1945, California ranked among the ten leading states in industrial employment.[10]

Until 1942, this tremendous increase in manufacturing did not create conditions conducive to a mass migration of Blacks. The combination of a growing demand for workers and an increasingly chronic shortage in the local labor supply finally caused war plants to hire large numbers of Blacks. The labor shortage became increasingly severe after 1941. Although the War Manpower Commission transferred approximately 800,000 workers to California by mid-1943, the state's need for employees was not filled until the end of the war.[11]

Los Angeles suffered one of the most acute manpower problems of any part of the nation. While industrial expansion created approximately 550,000 new jobs between 1940 and mid-1943, over 150,000 of its men entered the armed services. In the first nine months of 1942 aircraft plants lost nearly 20,000 workers through the draft and enlistments, and a spokesman for the industry predicted that Southern California plants would be "denuded of experienced workmen in the draft age group by the end of 1942."[12] In the face of such labor shortages, industries relaxed their hiring restrictions. Many women entered production jobs. In October, 1942, Consolidated Aircraft Company announced it would place "all individuals regardless of age or physical handicap." The Douglas firm put out advertisements in Spanish for Mexican workers.[13] Such a desperate hunt for workers could not sustain the exclusion of Blacks from military production jobs, and the bars to employment rapidly gave way to extensive job opportunities during 1942.

Having gained entry to the major war industries, Blacks composed a growing proportion of their workers until the end of 1944. They were hired extensively in shipyards. Black employment at the California Shipbuilding Company and Consolidated Steel yards increased from a few hundred in the spring of 1942 to 5,600 by November, 1943 and 7,022 by the end of 1944. The increasing proportion of the jobs obtained by Blacks may be seen in one yard which, between May and November, 1943, increased its Black employees from 2,474 to 4,076. By December, 1944, Blacks made up 14.7 percent and 11.0 percent of the California Shipbuilding Company and Consolidated Steel workers.[14]

Blacks also gained many jobs in the aircraft industry, although they composed a smaller proportion of the total work force. Lockheed-Vega employed approximately 600 Blacks in August, 1942; by April, 1943 its plants had over 2,500. In July, 1944, Los Angeles aircraft companies contained 7,186 Blacks composing from 3.2 to 7.2 percent of the workers in various firms.[15] Blacks obtained a limited number of jobs in some industries which had rigidly excluded them prior to 1942, such as the rubber companies. More training facilities were made available to them; by February, 1943, they composed over 12 percent of the trainees in government sponsored programs in Los Angeles County.[16]

Not all Blacks who came to Los Angeles found work in defense production, because discriminatory hiring and promotion practices continued for the duration of the war. Many trained Blacks could only obtain janitorial or other menial jobs and they comprised a disproportionately large number of workers on night shifts. Excluded from whole sections of some plants or segregated into special areas, Blacks did not gain jobs that gave them authority over White workers. They were largely excluded from higher paying positions of responsibility and received a disproportionately small number of jobs, compared to the size of their population. Neither the United States Employment Service nor the War Manpower Commission made a vigorous effort to secure jobs for Blacks where management objected to employing them, and the Fair Employment Practice Committee investigated only a few of the cases of discriminatory practice in Los Angeles.[17]

Some unions also followed discriminatory policies in hiring or promoting Blacks. The Association of Street, Electric Railway, and Motor Coach Operators, through strikes and strike threats, forced the Los Angeles Railway Company to restrict Black to jobs as janitors and coach cleaners. Despite a growing shortage of conductors and motormen, no Blacks were upgraded to those jobs until the FEPC ordered their promotion in August, 1944.[18] Several American Federation of Labor unions continued to bar Blacks from membership. However, the pressure of labor shortages finally led the International Association of Machinists to relax its objections to the employment of Blacks in aircraft plants.[19] The International Association of Boilermakers, however, continued to compel Blacks to join segregated auxiliary locals in which they had no voice in selecting officers or allocating jobs. Until 1943, this discrimination resulted in most of them securing employment as common laborers; few were promoted to higher paying jobs. In July of that year Black workers began a protest campaign, refused to pay dues until they were incorporated into the main local, and the companies fired over 300 of them. A subsequent Fair Employment Practice Commission investigation criticized both the companies and the Boilermakers for the auxiliary union policy but failed to end it. In 1944, however, the California Supreme Court declared segregated unions in a closed shop unconstitutional (James v. Marinship Corp., et al.), and they were gradually abandoned.[20]

In contrast to these practices, many unions followed policies which greatly improved the economic condition of Blacks in Los Angeles. The Congress of Industrial Organizations adopted a stand against racial discrimination, and became a leading force in breaking barriers to Black employment. By 1943, it had brought them into all main aircraft plants and rubber factories and had ended the segregated shops of the North American Company. Many AFL unions did not have segregated auxiliaries on the West Coast, and Black members enjoyed equal privileges with Whites which they did not enjoy in many other sections of the country.[21] Some unions with discriminatory membership conditions tried to change them such as the locals of the Machinists Union in Los Angeles which, by 1946, abandoned the racial features of their initiation ritual. Furthermore, few union discriminations seriously affected the availability of jobs to Blacks. Transportation workers composed a tiny fragment of the labor force. Black grievances against the Boilermakers were largely psychological and they were hired in large numbers in all shipyards where after mid-1943 they received frequent promotions.[22] It is doubtful that the discriminatory practices of some unions were a significant factor in discouraging migrants. It is unquestionable that the anti-discrimination activities of others made the condition of Blacks in Los Angeles more attractive.

The economic condition for Blacks in California and Los Angeles during World War II seemed especially inviting when compared with other sections of the nation. Few areas experienced greater industrial expansion or so acute a shortage of manpower; hence, few manufacturing centers offered such extensive job opportunities Blacks had a larger share of defense production jobs in relation to their population in California than in Southern urban areas. By December, 1944, they composed 6.5 percent of the total population in Los Angeles and in San Francisco-Oakland, but 14 percent of all shipyard workers. In the Gulf Coast states they made up nearly one-third of the inhabitants, but only 14 percent of the shipyard workers. Their representation in aircraft plants remained much nearer to their proportion of the population in Los Angeles than in Southern cities.[23] California also offered Blacks a greater chance to gain higher quality jobs:

> In general, the employment policies of Maritime
> yards in the Northeast and on the West Coast were
> sufficiently flexible to permit a considerable
> utilization of nonwhites in a wide variety of
> skills. On the other hand, very little progress
> in upgrading Negroes were made in the Southern
> and Gulf yards. With few exceptions, the yards
> south of Virginia utilized Negroes in a limited
> number of occupations, most of which were unskilled.[24]

During the World War II, California also offered the highest wage and income standards in the nation. Per capita income payments in the Golden State were $1,214 or 141.2 percent of the national average in 1942, and rose to a peak of $1,570 or 137.4 percent in 1944. Such a high average income was particularly attractive to residents of Southern states, where per capita income remained considerably below the national average. A similar gap existed between Los Angeles and Southern cities in industrial wages. Garment workers in 1945 averaged between 92 cents and $1.33 per hour in Los Angeles, as opposed to earnings of 44 cents to 62 cents per hour in the West South Central States. Ferrous foundry workers made 30 cents an hour more in Los Angeles than in the West South Central States. A larger wage differential existed between Los Angeles and Southeastern States.[25] Many Blacks found the gap between their earnings in California and in Southern states even greater than these averages indicate. They often advanced from domestic servants to common laborers in civilian industry to production workers in defense plants by migrating and thus increased their income several fold.

Contraction of the labor market at the end of World War II throughout the nation reduced economic opportunities for Blacks in California. From the surrender of Japan to the Korea War, California had a rate of unemployment considerably higher than the nation as a whole. The numbers out of work reached a peak of 485,000 or 9.2 percent of the civilian labor force in April, 1944, and it never declined below 6.7 percent during the entire post war period. The national rate varied from 3.9 percent.[26] As in other regions, Blacks composed a disproportionate share of California's jobless. Largely unskilled laborers with low seniority suffered most in those industries which they had depended upon for production: Shipbuilding, aircraft, and electronics. Defense plants in Portland, Oregon released 50 percent of their Black workers by September, 1945; those in San Francisco reduced them by 25 percent.[27]

The postwar boom in civilian industries did not offer Blacks promising job opportunities. An increased supply of labor permitted a revival of discriminatory hiring practices which kept many of those dismissed from war industries out of work for long periods. Attempts to remove it in 1946 failed. Southern filibustering blocked the Congressional Fair Employment Practices bill; California's version failed to pass both houses of the legislature and was rejected by the electorate as an initiative. In the recession at the end of the decade, Blacks continued to compose a disproportionate share of the unemployed. Of the state's total labor force, 339,600 or 8.5 percent were without jobs; of its Black workers, 41,925 or 14.2 percent were unemployed.[28]

During the postwar period, Blacks had difficulty obtaining employment in all parts of the country. They faced discrimination in hiring and promotion in all states and were more concentrated in service and common labor jobs in many Southern states than in California.[29] Thus, the economic condition of Blacks in California after 1944 presented a puzzling picture of disappointment for its new Black residents, compared to opportunities at the peak of war, combined with dissatisfaction when contrasted with conditions in other states.

A survey of the United States Employment Services in February, 1946, reported "a higher percentage of discrimination than had ever previously been recorded."[30] Blacks found nearly all clerical and commercial jobs in private firms closed to them. The number hired in the skilled trades was so small that many Blacks were discouraged from training for them. Employment opportunities were further reduced by competition from Japanese-Americans who returned from relocation camps to take many jobs which had been historically reserved for nonwhites.[31]

On the other hand, Blacks did not lose all of their war-time employment gains. The majority of those who obtained jobs in military production industries during World War II retained them. Losses of employment in oil refineries and heavy industries were balanced by gains in government agencies and the food industry.[32] While many Blacks entering civilian industries worked as janitors, domestic servants, or unskilled laborers, approximately one-third of them were placed in manufacturing jobs. A few entered long-closed skilled or clerical jobs. In 1947 Los Angeles became one of the few cities in the nation in which Blacks found employment as conductors on public transit lines and as telephone operators. Public training facilities remained open; they were not relegated to pre-war conditions of being unable to secure employment or training. Their efforts to enter new plants, sometimes aided by unions, proved successful as in the case of a General Motors assembly plant which voluntarily hired Blacks in July, 1946.[33]

At the end of the decade, however, Blacks in Los Angeles still composed a disproportionately large number of workers in lower status jobs and those out of work. The caliber of their jobs gave them a median income considerably lower than that of whites and less in comparison to other cities than during World War II.[34]

The importance of economic growth in attracting Blacks to Los Angeles during World War II is undeniable. Black migration in the postwar period, however, is more difficult to explain in terms of employment opportunities. The rates of unemployment in California and Los Angeles remained among the highest in the nation. Even so, very few wartime migrants left these areas, and a steady stream continued to enter them. The lack of alternative employment was certainly one reason for most Blacks remaining in California, but this is an adequate explanation for their continued movement into the state. Interviews with migrants who came to Los Angeles during the postwar period revealed that economic conditions were of negligible importance in shaping their decision to move; their reasons were primarily non-economic.[35] In accounting for Black migration to California and Los Angeles, especially during the second half of the 1940's, other factors must be considered in addition to economic conditions.

Many Blacks moved to California with little knowledge of the job opportunities or income it offered. Some were attracted by the climate and the widespread publicity about it. During the postwar years, the Chambers of Commerce and tourist clubs advertised the area as widely as in the 1920's. The image of Southern California as a land of sunshine and wealth continued to draw White and Black migrants, including a large number of tourists, some of whom decided to stay. A considerable number responded to hearsay alone; they had never visited the state nor read about it, but they "heard it was great" and so resolved to visit or move to it. Many Black servicemen, stationed in Los Angeles area during the war, returned with their families. They composed a significant portion of the in-migration immediately after the war when mounting unemployment reduced the economic attractiveness of California cities.[36]

Many Blacks who left Southern states in quest of greater freedom and social equality chose to move to Los Angeles or other California cities. Neither Los Angeles nor San Francisco had widespread reputations for residential segregation until the end of the decade. Nor had these cities experienced anti-Black riots of the magnitude that struck Chicago or Detroit during World War II. Other Blacks, especially those in professions or middle income jobs moved from the South Los Angeles to provide more equal educational opportunities for their children. Most of them remained in spite of the greater difficulties they faced in entering a profession or securing a position in business.[37]

The prior movements of Blacks to Los Angeles also hastened the influx of the 1940's. A sample survey of migrants to Los Angeles revealed that over half of those who came during the war and nearly all who arrived after 1945 had friends or family in the city. Personal contacts were especially important during World War II as a source of housing for newcomers in the seriously congested Black community. The residence of one "trail blazer" in Los Angeles often attracted several other family members and sometimes a number of neighbors. However, the Black press in Los Angeles gave little encouragement to Southerners to move to Los Angeles, and resident Blacks did not always welcome them.[38]

Many who came to Los Angeles seeking relief from Southern discrimination encountered disappointment, especially during World War II.

The housing, recreation, education, and transportation facilities of the city were inadequate to fill the needs of the rapidly growing Black population. Competition for existing facilities produced inter-racial tensions. A representative of the Committee for Congested Production Areas reported of Los Angeles in April, 1944:

> For several months there has been a bad racial
> problem seething beneath the surface in this...
> This feeling has come to the surface several
> times in the past, and at the moment is out in
> the open because of the unwillingness of our
> local transportation company to employ Negroes
> as platform workers on their streetcars.[39]

Some observers attributed such feelings largely to the influx of Southern Blacks. They were considered "inferior" to other citizens, often illiterate, and prone to spend their earnings on liquor or nar-cotics.[40] Demands mounted to stop their entrance to Los Angeles as a means of easing the problems of wartime congestion. In November, 1943, Los Angeles Deputy Mayor Orville R. Caldwell warned a subcommittee of House Naval Affairs Committee:

> The Negro who was born and reared here fits into
> our picture, but these Southern Negroes are a
> serious problem. They don't get along with the
> Negroes who were born and reared here, nor with
> the white residents...If this in-migration is
> not stopped, until such time as these people can
> be properly absorbed into the community, dire
> results will insue.[41]

In response to such criticisms, the subcommittee recommended that the War Manpower Commission limit the number of Blacks recruited for service in Los Angeles.[42]

The most serious problem Blacks met in Los Angeles - inadequate housing facilities - was too deeply rooted and complex to be relieved by simply reducing recruitment of Black workers. Blacks had been restricted to approximately 5 percent of the residential area of the city by rigid segregation policies, and this area was heavily inhabited by 1940 and little expansion of housing facilities took place during the war. By the end of 1943, the Black population had doubled, but was still forced to dwell in essentially the same area, many of the buildings were substandard.[43] The one additional section to which Blacks gained access was "Little Tokyo" after most of its Japanese residents had been relocated in interior states. Renamed "Bronzeville," this area rapidly filled up and became the worst example of congestion in the city. The chairman of the Los Angeles City Housing Authority reported in the summer of 1943 that "Little Tokyo" had become a "Black ghetto" and that many families lived in makeshift residences without

sanitary facilities.[44] A few months later, a member of the City
Housing Authority illustrated some conditions in one area:

> Records of our applications show families piling
> up to a congestion of four, five, and six persons
> per bedroom. In one case a family of five was
> living in a dirt-floored garage with no sanitary
> facilities whatsoever. In an abandoned store
> front and two nearly windowless storage rooms in
> Little Tokyo twenty-one people were found to be
> living - and paying $50 a month for these quarters.[45]

Despite chronic overcrowding, steadily worsened by in-migration,
no relaxation occurred in residential segregation and the amount of
new housing available to Blacks remained limited throughout the war.
Residential segregation steadily tightened during the early 1940's
as White property owners secured the limited supply of housing outside
existing Black areas for White occupancy only by attaching restrictive
covenants to the titles. In several areas real estate interest and
"home improvement" associations led vigorous campaigns to cover all
residential structures with covenants. By this method, much of the
San Gabriel Valley and Pasadena became closed to Blacks in 1941.[46]
The Maywood-Bell Southeast Herald newspaper appealed to the citizens
to adopt covenants and illustrated the apprehension with which many
Whites viewed the entry of Blacks to their neighborhoods:

> Within the next few weeks one section of the com-
> munity is definitely threatened with the moving
> in of undesireables for race restriction run out
> in this...
>
> Up to now your child...could attend...school with-
> out fear of having to mix with undesirables...It
> would not be fair to subject them to the humilia-
> tion and deprivation which mixed races would force
> upon them.[47]

Although challenged by Blacks, courts upheld the covenants as a
means of preventing Black occupancy of housing until 1945.
The shortage of housing available to Blacks was not substantially
relieved by new construction. The shortage of materials and military
priorities on building supplies reduced the number of units built
during the war. Most construction took place in areas outside Black
section, and both the landlords and real estate agents adopted the
prevailing restrictions on nonwhite occupancy. Few contractors attempted to open project to all races and those who did often closed
them after pressure from White citizens.[48]
Government financed construction of dwelling units was opposed
in Los Angeles throughout the war in spite of the need for additional

housing. Real estate men regarded it as a threat to private enterprise, and many business-related interests joined them in restricting the amount of locally financed public housing to a few thousand units. Blacks are further denied relief through this channel by the policies of the Los Angeles City Housing Authority to restrict Blacks to a quota of housing constructed and not to open units outside the Black area to their occupancy.[49] In several cases Blacks had to wage strong campaigns against associations of White residents to gain entrance to projects erected around the fringe of the Black community. In their quest for housing they received no encouragement from the city council, several members of which are avowed proponents of segregation.[50]

The widespread use of restrictive covenants and the limited availability of new housing units left Blacks with the most chronic housing situation of any group in Los Angeles. In the Fall of 1943, the City Housing Authority had 1,795 applications for housing from Blacks as opposed to 362 from Whites, 238 from Mexicans and 5 from other minority groups.[51] This shortage became the major source to racial tension, breeding problems beyond the scope of housing congestion. Howard Holtzendorf told the Izak Subcommittee:

> The City Health Officer has stated...that a disease
> epidemic involving the whole Southern California
> was plant area might be caused by this congestion
> (in Negro areas); the Chief of Police has stated
> that the situation is of 'momentous concern'; the
> Chief Fire Engineer has stated 'the possibility of
> a confligration in the entire (Negro) area is very
> high.' In addition the possibility of race riot
> nurtured by subversive elements within the community
> and fed by the mal-content that exists because of
> this intolerable housing condition cannot be over-
> looked.[52]

Racial tension, congested living conditions, journalistic publicity, and the belligerent public attitude all contributed to the one major race riot which Los Angeles experienced. Unlike riots in other cities in 1943, it did not center on the Black population, but Mexicans during the so-called zoot-suit riots. Congested living quarters and a lack of recreational facilities led many minority group youths to organize in gangs and to find an outlet for their feelings in delinquent activity, including attacks on servicemen. On the night of June 3, a group of sailors clashed with some zoot-suiters, and other servicemen quickly joined the melee. From then until June 7, the Mexican sections of the city were raided by sailors, marines, and soldiers, and a large number of Mexicans as well as some Blacks suffered beatings. Police did little to restrain the servicemen until June 7, and sporadic clashes took place between servicemen and Blacks in Watts and Pasadena through June 13.[53]

Racial tension continued in various forms for the duration of the

war. The exclusion of Blacks from jobs as conductors on city streetcars and the inadequacy of transportation facilities in Black districts
contributed to several incidents of violence between Whites and Blacks
aboard streetcars. The most serious took place in May, 1944, when over
100 Black youths mobbed a trolley and beat several White passengers.[54]
The large migration of Whites from Southern states augmented the friction as they resisted the hiring and promotion of Blacks in many industries such as the shipyards. Ku Klux Klan activity underwent a considerable revival in Los Angeles during the 1940's as a result of the
influx both of Blacks and of Southern Whites.[55] All friction, of course,
was not interracial. Many Blacks, who had resided in Los Angeles for a
considerable period, looked down upon newcomers from Southern states
as undisciplined, boisterous, tactless, and prone to lawless activity.
The California Eagle attributed the enlarged crime wave in the Black
community largely to Southern migrants, and many older residents tried
to segregate them as fully as Whites did.[56]

Blacks in Los Angeles continued to experience discriminations and
interracial tension during the postwar period. An official in the
National Association for the Advancement of Colored People noted in
April, 1946:

> The influx of southern (sic) Whites here, who bring
> with them their provincial and distorted racial
> views, in my opinion is directly the cause of this
> new friction. Secondly, southern (sic) Blacks, who
> have moved here in large numbers, haven't helped
> the situation any. Generally speaking, they have
> gone from one extreme, that of being almost com-
> pletely suppressed in the south (sic), to the other
> extreme, that of taking advantage of comparative
> freedom by unnecessary bulldozing tactics in their
> relationship with other groups.[57]

However, incidents of interracial friction in 1946 cannot be
attributed to migrants from any one area. It reflected a rather
reaction to the change in the employment opportunities for Blacks and
particularly their efforts to expand their residential facilities.
During the first months following the end of World War II, the
Black housing shortage threatened to become more acute when thousands
of Japanese returned from relocation camps and sought their former
homes in "Little Tokyo". The first incident occurred when a Buddhist
priest tried to evict 75 Blacks housed in his temple, in December 1944.
Similar attempts by Japanese to regain property occupied by Blacks
provoked robberies against their stores and homes in an effort to dis-
courage their return to Los Angeles.[58] At the same time, Blacks
increased their drive to penetrate covenanted areas by a series of
court cases, and, in some instances, encountered violence. In the
first six months of 1946, ten Black families who had entered White
neighborhoods had crosses burned on their lawns.[59]

Several factors gradually relaxed the enforcement of covenants after 1945, which lessened housing congestion and racial tensions. Courts began to change their attitudes on enforcing covenants. In the celebrated "Sugar Hill" case, Judge Thurmond Clark rejected race covenants as contrary to the Fourteenth Amendment. Other demands for enforcement were turned down on the grounds that the composition of the neighborhood had changed from all-White to mixed races, eliminating the basic purpose of the covenants. The final legal blow to excluding Blacks through covenants came in 1948 when the Supreme Court of the United States declared them unenforceable in Shelly v. Kramer.[60] The construction of new housing for Whites also opened restricted areas to Blacks. By 1947 many realtors were glad to admit Blacks to older neighborhoods previously closed; over half of the city's Blacks resided in houses which had race restrictive covenants attached to their titles. Community resistance, however, continued to prevent Blacks from securing homes in some parts of Los Angeles city and in most suburban areas.[61]

The end of the housing shortage reduced racial tension, but Blacks continued to meet many discriminations. They encountered them less frequently than in Southern states, but this only increased the frustrations of some migrants. Relations between Blacks and police officers became the leading source of friction. Blacks found alone at night were often taken to jail on charges of vagrancy, and reports of violent treatment of arrested Blacks continued throughout the postwar period. On the other hand, Los Angeles had a comparatively good record of race relations after the war. Carey McWilliams noted in 1948:

> Police brutality continues to be a major irritant to group relations in Los Angeles with 'incidents' occuring...that have unquestionably aggravated, as they have also reflected, increasing tension in certain areas. There is probably less miscellaneous Jim Crowism in Los Angeles than in any city in the West and, certainly, there is less discrimination in places of public accomodation than in 1940...Today there is a minimum of discrimination in hotels, restaurants, stores, and places of amusement and entertainment, that is, a minimum by comparison with other west coast cities. The general situation in the schools can also be said to reflect some slight improvement in teacher attitudes, administration policies, and, more particularly, in a new interest which has been created in majority-minority relations.[62]

Incidents of racial friction in Los Angeles do not appear to have influenced the volume of Black migration. The zoot-suit riot occurred at the peak of the wartime boom; during the two succeeding months the number of migrants entering Los Angeles changed little. Since the violence was not directed primarily against Blacks it did not stigmatize the city as a place of Black-White conflict such as riots and bombings in Detroit and Chicago. The housing shortage one principal local problem aggravated by Black migration, did not reduce its volume. Housing had already become congested by 1943, yet Blacks continued to come to Los Angeles in growing numbers. No evidence indicates that the decline in migration after the summer of 1943 was connected with the chronic residential problem. These gestures of racial tension were outweighted in the minds of many Blacks by an image of Los Angeles as an area comparatively free from discrimination. In the postwar period the lessening of racial friction, housing congestion, and discrimination perpetuated this impression and encouraged most of the wartime migrants to remain.

The large movement of Blacks to Los Angeles between 1942 and 1950 represented the culmination of several decades of gradually rising in-migration. The stream which had moved there since the early 1900's, substantial in volume but insignificant in relation to the influx of Whites, assumed the proportions of a flood after mid-1942. Blacks became conspicuous migrants for the first time. By 1950 they composed an important segment of the city's population, and Los Angeles gained a place among the leading centers of Blacks in the nation. Ironically, however, the movement which brought Los Angeles' Black community to such a size also lessened its singular importance within California. Their numbers spread to several cities in the state and by 1950 the San Francisco-Oakland area rivaled Los Angeles to a characteristic of the leading metropolitan area of the state. Within each metropolitan area, of course, there had developed a distinctive Black community, shaped largely by the wartime experience. Watts was such a community.

FOOTNOTES

1 Census of Population: 1950, II, Part 5, 97-103; Census of Population: 1950, IV, Part 4, Chap. B, 100: U.S. Bureau of the Census, Seventeenth Census of the United States, Census of Population: 1950, Vol. II, Characteristics of the Population, Part 37 (Washington, 1952), p. 51; Seventeen Census of the United States, Census of Population: 1950, Vol. II, Characteristics of the Population, Part 47 (Washington, 1952), p. 67.

2 Population - Characteristics, Series CA-3, No. 3, p. 8; U.S. Bureau of the Census, Population - Special Censuses, Series P-SC, No. 97 (Washington, December 5, 1945); Population - Special Censuses, Series P-28, No. 280 (Washington, January 23, 1948). Hereafter cited as Population - Special Censuses, Series P-SC, Nos. 81, 97, Series P-28, No. 280, 261-262.

3 Census of Population: 1950, II, Part 5, 96; Sixteenth Census, Population, II, Part I, 516-517; Census of Population: 1950, IV, Part 4, Chap. B, 100; Cy Wilson Record, "Willie Stokes at Golden Gate, Crisis, LVI (June, 1949), 187.

[4] U.S. Congress, House, Subcommittee of the Committee on Naval Affairs, Hearings, Investigations of Congested Areas, 87th Congress, 1st Session, Part 8, 1943, pp. 1763-1767. Hereafter cited as House Committee on Naval Affairs, Hearings, Izak Subcommittee; California Eagle, August 20, 1942, pp. 1-A, 5-A; October 8, 1942, p. 5-A. The failure of the Southern Pacific Railroad Company to hire many of the imported Negroes left a large number homeless and unemployed in Los Angeles and strained city and state relief and emergency housing facilities. A committee was established in July, 1942, headed by Carey McWilliams, to investigate the railroad and the resultant, social and economic problems caused by the mass importations. California Eagle, August 6, 1942, p. 1-A; Carey McWilliams, "The Los Angeles Archipelago," Science and Society, X (Winter, 1946), p. 52.

[5] Population - Characteristics, Series CA-3, No. 3, p. 8; U.S. Bureau of the Census, Population - Special Censuses, Series P-SC No. 188 (Washington, October 29, 1946), p. 8.

[6] Population - Special Censuses, Series P-SC, No. 188; Census of Population: 1950, II, Part 5, 100; Census of Population: 1950, IV, Part 4, Chap. B, 33, 93, 100.

[7] See Ante, pp. 261-262.

[8] Census of Population: 1950, II, Part 5, pp. 97-104, 162.

[9] Sixteenth Census, Population, II, Part 1, 516-617; Census of Population: 1950, II, Part 5, p. 100.

[10] California Eagle, March 17, 1943, p. 3-A; "Regional Differences in Jobs, Income, and Migration, 1929-49," Monthly Labor Review LXXI (October, 1950), p. 433; Los Angeles Times, October 20, 1943; House Committee on Naval Affairs, Hearings, Izak Subcommittee, Part 8, p. 1987; Margaret S. Gordon, Employment Expansion and Population Growth, 108-109.

[11] "Labor in California and the Pacific Northwest," Monthly Labor Review, LXIV (April, 1947), 565; U.S. Office of War Information, "Migration of War Workers During the Last Three and a Half Years," Advance Release for Wednesday Morning Papers, April 19, 1944. From the John A. Davis Files, FEPC Records, National Archives.

[12] House Committee on Naval Affairs, Hearings, Izak Subcommittee, Part 8, p. 1987; Los Angeles Times, November 8, 1942; U.S. Congress, House, Select Committee Investigating National Defense Migration, Hearings, National Defense Migration, 77th Congress, 1st Session, Part 34, 1942, p. 13097. Heareafter cited as House Committee Investigating National Defense Migration, Hearings on National Defense Migration.

13 Los Angeles Times, June 7, 1942; October 27, 1942; December 15, 1942.

14 "Nonwhite Employment in Selected West Coast Shipbuilding Establishments, November, 1943" (n.p., n.d.). Davis Files, FEPC Records, National Archives; Council of Social Agencies, Los Angeles, "Preliminary Review and Recommendations Regarding Employment Problems of Minorities during the Reconversion Period" (n.p., August 29, 1944), p. 2; U.S. Fair Employment Practice Committee, "Hearings on the Matter of Western Pipe and Steel Company...and Auxiliary Lodge A-35...Brotherhood of Boilermakers" (n.p., November 19, 1943), pp. 246-247. From the Legal Division Files, FEPC Records, National Archives.

15 Council of Social Agencies, loc. cit.; U.S. Office of War Information, loc. cit.; House Committee Investigating National Defense Migration, Hearings on National Defense Migration, Part 34, pp. 13253-54; Robert C. Weaver, "Negro Employment in the Aircraft Industry," Quarterly Journal of Economics, LIX (August, 1945), pp. 609-10, 616-17.

16 California Eagle, February 24, 1943, p. 4-A; Letter from Selma Sorin, California State Department of Social Welfare, to Margaret S. Watkins, November 20, 1942.

17 Weaver, op. cit., pp. 616-17; Council of Social Agencies, op. cit., pp. 2-3.

18 California Eagle, March 3, 1943, p. 1-A; U.S. Fair Employment Practice Committee, Final Report (Washington, 1947), p. 15; FEPC, "Hearings in re...Los Angeles Railway Corporation," pp. 214-15. The refusal of transportation workers' unions to allow Blacks to serve as conductors or operators was not a problem unique to Los Angeles during World War II. In January, 1944 FEPC investigated a similar situation in Philadelphia's public transit companies, and on August 1, it ordered the promotion of eight Blacks to motormen over the objections of the union. This action led to the walkout of 5,000 white workers that paralyzed the city's transportation facilities for five days and grew into minor race riot. The week after this incident, FEPC held its Los Angeles hearings, and managers of the Los Angeles Railway Corporation warned that a similar reaction would occur in Los Angeles if Blacks were upgraded. However, the union took no action against Blacks when they were given jobs as operators in September, and by May, 1945, 124 Blacks had been promoted. Los Angeles Times, August 2, 1944; August 5, 1944; August 9, 1944.

19 California Eagle, July 29, 1943, p. 1-A.

20 Los Angeles Times, July 23, 1943; FEPC, Final Report, pp. 12-21; Daniel R. Donovan and James Wolfe, "Report in pursuance of investigation...by the...President's Committee on Fair Employment Practice," pp. 10-11, 22, Davis Files, FEPC Reports, National Archives; U.S.

Fair Employment Practice Committee, "Summary, Findings, and Directives Relating to California Shipbuilding Company...International Brotherhood of Boilermakers...Auxiliary Lodge A-35" (n.p., December 9, 1943), Legal Division Files, FEPC Records, National Archives. See also Fred Stripp, "The Treatment of Negro-American Workers by the AFL and CIO in the San Francisco Bay Area," Social Forces, XXVIII (March, 1950), 330-32.

[21] California Eagle, January 8, 1943, pp. 1-A, 5-A; January 28, 1943, p. 5-A; Scott Greer, "The Participation of Ethnic Minorities in the Labor Unions of Los Angeles County" (Unpublished Ph.D. dissertation, University of California, Los Angeles, 1952), p. 70.

[22] Daniel R. Donovan and James Wolfe, "Report in Pursuance of Investigation by the President's Committee on Fair Employment Practice" (Washington, 1947), pp. 13-15. California Eagle, February 24, 1943, p. 7-B; April 18, 1946, p. 3; FEPC, "Hearings in re Western Pipe and Steel," pp. 93-95.

[23] FEPC, Final Report, pp. 27-28; Robert C. Weaver, Quarterly Journal of Economics, LIX, "Negro Employment in the Aircraft Industry," (August, 1945), pp. 616-617.

[24] U.S. Fair Employment Practice Committee, Final Report (Washington, 1947), p. 27.

[25] "Labor in the South II - Income in the South," Monthly Labor Review, LXIII (October, 1946), pp. 497, 513; Monthly Labor Review, LXIV, pp. 601, 611.

[26] Monthly Labor Review, LXIV (April, 1947), "Labor in California and Pacific Northwest," pp. 561-695; Margaret Gordon, Employment Expansion and Economic Growth, The California Experience: 1900-1950 (Berkeley, 1954), pp. 1-2, 181.

[27] U.S. Fair Employment Practice Committee, "Impact of Reconversion on Minority Workers" (Washington, n.d.), pp. 7-9. FEPC Records, National Archives.

[28] Ibid., p. 28; California Eagle, February 14, 1946, p. 2.

[29] Census of Population: 1950, II, Part 1, 413-414; Census of Population: 1950, II, Part 5, p. 463.

[30] Harold Draper, Jim Crow in Los Angeles (Pamphlet published by the Worker's Party, Los Angeles, 1946), p. 9. Los Angeles Times, December 19, 1945.

[31] FEPC, "Impact of Reconversion on Minority Workers," p. 11; FEPC, Final Report, p. 82; statement by Dr. Hampton B. Howes on the

employment status of Blacks in Los Angeles, April, 1946. From the files of the Los Angeles County Commission on Human Rights.

[32] Statement by Dr. Hampton B. Howes; FEPC, Final Report, pp. 81-82.

[33] National Conference of Social Work, Proceedings of the 74th Annual Conference (San Francisco, 1947), pp. 89-91; California Eagle, July 11, 1946, p. 1.

[34] Census of Population: 1950, II, Part 1, 456; Census of Population: 1950, II, Part 5, pp. 258-262, 250-253.

[35] Oral Interviews with Blacks who moved to Los Angeles during 1940's, Los Angeles, California, August, 1973.

[36] Ibid.

[37] Ibid.

[38] Ibid.

[39] Charles B. Spaulding, "Housing Problems of Minority Groups in Los Angeles County," The Annals of the American Academy of Political and Social Science, CCXLVI (November, 1946), pp. 220-221.

[40] House Committee on Naval Affairs, Hearings, Izak Subcommittee, Part 8, p. 1764.

[41] Ibid., p. 1761.

[42] Los Angeles Times, December 3, 1943.

[43] California Eagle, December 11, 1942, p. 8-A; Statement of Howard L. Holtzendorf before Izak Subcommittee of the House Naval Affairs Committee investigating war housing conditions in Los Angeles, November 10, 1943. Los Angeles Area Files, CCPA Records, National Archives. Hereafter cited as statement of Holtzendorf before Izak Subcommittee. A complete discussion of the Negro housing problem in Los Angeles, with it multifold ramifications in the politics, law, social thought, and economy of the area, would require a dissertation in itself. The following discussion can only touch on a few of the outstanding features and developments of the problem during the 1940's. For a fuller treatment see Robert C. Weaver, Negro Ghetto (New York, 1948); Charles B. Spaulding, "Housing Problems of Minority Groups in Los Angeles County," The Annals of the American Academy of Political and Social Service, CCXLVIII (November, 1946), pp. 220-225. The issue of race restrictive covenants is treated in Charles S. Johnson and Herman H. Long, People vs. Property (Nashville, 1947); D.O. McGovney, "Racial Residential Segregation by State Court Enforcement of Restrictive Agreements,

Covenants, or Conditions in Deeds in Unconstitutional," <u>California Law Review</u>, XXXIII (March, 1945), pp. 5-39. Residential segregation is most clearly illustrated by census tract statistics. See U.S. Bureau of the Census, Sixteenth Census of the United States: 1940, <u>Population and Housing</u>, Statistics for Census Tracts, Los Angeles - Long Beach, California (Washington, 1942); <u>Population - Special Reports</u>, Series P-SC, No. 188; U.S. Bureau of the Census, <u>Census of Housing:</u> <u>1950</u>, Vol. V, <u>Block Statistics</u>, No. 100 (Washington, 1952).

Block Statistics, No. 100 (Washington, 1952). Negro housing conditions in San Francisco during World War II are treated in Charles S. Johnson, <u>The Negro War Worker in San Francisco</u> (San Francisco, 1944).

[44] <u>California Eagle</u>, August 5, 1943, p. 5-B.

[45] Statement of Howard L. Holtzendof before Izak Subcommittee of the House Naval Affairs Committee investigating war housing conditions in Los Angeles, November 10, 1943, Part 9, p. 1764. Hereafter cited as statement of Holtzendorf before Izak subcommittee. A complete discussion of the Black housing problem in Los Angeles, with its multifold ramifications in the politics, law, social thought, and economy during the war years, would require a dissertation in itself.

[46] <u>California Eagle</u>, October 23, 1941, pp. 1-A, 3-A.

[47] Quoted in <u>California Eagle</u>, March 26, 1942, p. 1-A.

[48] House Committee on Naval Affairs, <u>Hearings, Izak Subcommittee</u>, Part 8, pp. 1852-1853.

[49] <u>California Eagle</u>, January 8, 1943, pp. 1-A, 5-A; November 28, 1946, p. 1; Spaulding, <u>The Annals</u>, CCXLVIII, 223-224. Until the early months of 1943 the Los Angeles City Housing Authority restricted Blacks to 10 percent of the dwelling units erected. This ban was lifted in 1943, but neither city nor county housing projects gave the Black much relief from congestion since most of them were built outside of Black residential areas.

[50] <u>California Eagle</u>, October 28, 1943, pp. 1-A, 2-A; November 18, 1943, pp. 1-A, 2-A. The most outstanding battle over keeping out of public housing occurred in the Watts district in October, 1943, when White property owners formed the South Los Angeles Home Owners Association and applied pressure on the City Council to change the non-restricted status which the City Housing Authority had granted to a 465 unit project. Their campaign was met by a vigorous counter-campaign on the part of Blacks and the project remained open. However, the City Council showed its feelings on segregated housing by defeating a resolution to go on record as opposing race discrimination in the Watts project by a vote of 8 to 7.

[51] Statement of Holtzendorf before Izak Subcommittee.

[52] _Ibid_. The effects of housing congestion on disease and crime in the Black community are discussed in Myra R. Schapps, "The Effect of War and War Conditions on Minority Groups with Special Reference to the American Negro" (Unpublished report prepared for the State Department of Social Welfare, 1942).

[53] Jesse P. Guzman (ed.), _Negro Year Book_, 10th edition (Atlanta, 1947), pp. 236-237; Lucille Kennedy, "Information on Young Migrant Workers, Los Angeles Area" (Report prepared for the State Department of Social Welfare, 1944); _California Eagle_, June 6, 1943; pp. 1-A, 8-A; June 10, 1943, p. 1-A; June 17, 1943, p. 8-A; _Los Angeles Times_, June 3 to June 13, 1943; House Committee on Naval Affairs, _Hearings, Izak Subcommittee_, Part 8, p. 1770.

[54] _Los Angeles Times_, May 13, 1944; August 9, 1944; October 17, 1944.

[55] _California Eagle_, December 9, 1943, p. 16; May 6, 1943, p. 1-A; March 20, 1947, pp. 1, 8.

[56] The problems of adjustment which Blacks from the South met upon moving to Pacific Coast Division cities are treated in Eugene S. Richards' "Migration and the Social Education of the Negro," _Journal of Negro Education_ XIII (Winter, 1944), pp. 40-46. The reaction of resident Negroes to the Southern influx in Oregon and Washington is discussed in Robert E. Colbert's "The Attitude of Older Negro Residents Toward Recent Negro Migrants in the Pacific Northwest," _Journal of Negro Education_ XV (Fall, 1946).

[57] Quoted in _California Eagle_, April 4, 1946, p. 3.

[58] Charles B. Spaulding, "Housing Problems of Minority Groups in Los Angeles County," _The Annals of the American Academy of Political and Social Science_, CCXLVI (November, 1946), pp. 220-25; _Los Angeles Times_, December 31, 1944; March 4, 1947.

[59] _California Eagle_, July 17, 1947, p. 8; June 6, 1946, p. 2; May 23, 1946, p. 1.

[60] _Shelley v. Kramer_, 334 U.S. 72 (1948); _California Eagle_, September 5, 1946.

[61] Robert C. Weaver, _The Negro Ghetto_ (1948), pp. 7, 236; Carey McWilliams, "Los Angeles: An Emerging Pattern," _Common Ground_, IX (Spring, 1949), pp. 8-9.

[62] McWilliams, _Common Ground_, IX, p. 8.

CHAPTER 3

WATTS: MATURATION OF A GHETTO, 1940-1950

The entire region known as Watts was given to Anastacio Abila in 1843 by Governor Manuel Micheltorena as one of the Mexican land grants. The grant, comparatively small, received the Spanish name, Tajuata, meaning the low bluffs on the North.[1] Between 1843 and 1900, the population of the area grew tremendously; while its geographic perimeters remained basically the same. The area as we know it today developed as the Black population of the Central Avenue area moved South between 1920-1930.[2] A pictorial explanation of the historical development of the Watts community is illustrated in the map on the following page.

The Pacific Electric Railroad Company became a major factor in this development, not only as a means of transportation to jobs and markets in the city of Los Angeles and to recreation at the beaches, but as a source of employment as well. Workmen laying tracks for the Long Beach, Redondo Beach, San Pedro, and Santa Ana lines lived with their families in housing furnished by the railroad South of Watts Station. Watts was annexed to the city of Los Angeles in 1926. Its boundaries were 92nd Street on the North, Central Avenue on the West continuing to 108th Street and Success Avenue, Imperial Highway on the South and Mona Boulevard along 103rd Street to Crosesus on the East.[3] Between 1940 and 1950, Black migration into Watts increased at a rate which made it difficult to reverse.

Table I, as presented in Chapter I, illustrates the growth of the Black population between 1940 and 1950 in California. In the state, the Black population in 1940 was 124,306 or 1.8 percent of the total population.[4] In 1950, the Black population in California was 462,172 or 4.4 percent of the total population.[5] In other words, Blacks comprised 40 percent of the total non-White population in 1940 and 68.9 percent in 1950. By contrast, Los Angeles County's Black population was 75,209 in 1940 or 2.7 percent of the total population and 217,881 in 1950, or 5.2 percent of the total population.[6] These figures represent a striking comparison to the state and are further contrasted in Table IV which is found on a later page. The increase was dramatic; in fact, the state of California experienced a 2.6 percent increase in its Black population during the decade under discussion or a total of 337,866 persons. The county of Los Angeles alone experienced a 2.5 percent increase in the same decade or a total of 142,672 persons. Los Angeles county thus received more than one-third of the increase in the state's Black population.

The comparison becomes more striking when one includes the Black population in the city of Los Angeles. Table V, which follows Table IV, permits a state-county-city comparison by race in leading California cities during the 1940's. In 1940 the total Black population in the city of Los Angeles was 97,847. By 1950, it had reached 211,585. A

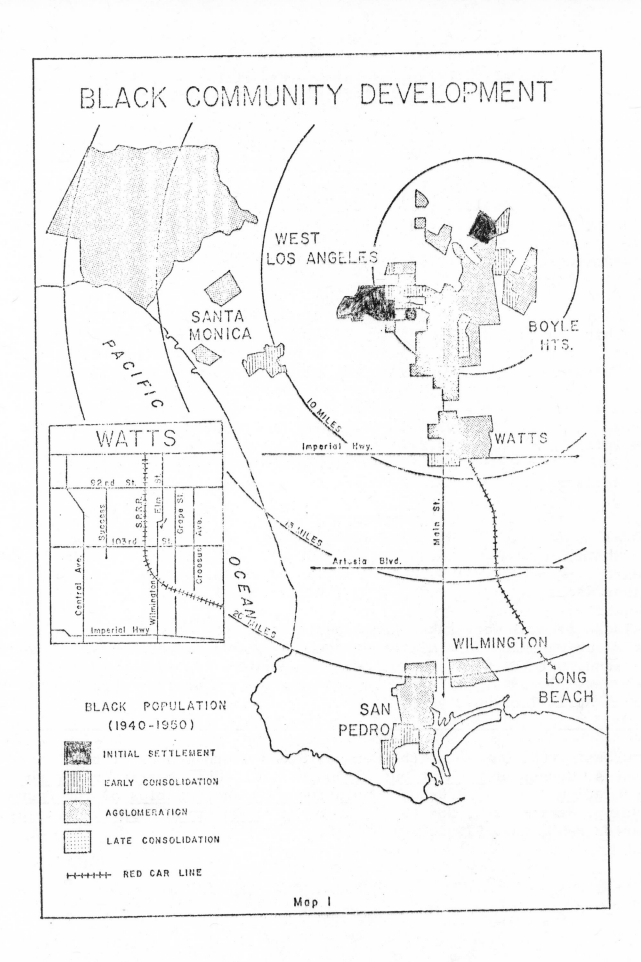

BLACK COMMUNITY DEVELOPMENT

WEST
LOS ANGELES

SANTA
MONICA

PACIFIC

BOYLE
HTS.

10 MILES

Imperial Hwy.

WATTS

Main St.

15 MILES

Artesia Blvd.

OCEAN

20 MILES

WILMINGTON

LONG
BEACH

SAN
PEDRO

WATTS

92nd St.

Success

S.P.R.R.

Elm St.

Grape St.

103rd St.

Central Ave.

Wilmington

Croesus Ave.

Imperial Hwy

BLACK POPULATION
(1940-1950)

INITIAL SETTLEMENT

EARLY CONSOLIDATION

AGGLOMERATION

LATE CONSOLIDATION

+++++++ RED CAR LINE

Map I

TABLE IV

POPULATION TRENDS IN LEADING CALIFORNIA CITIES
DURING THE 1940's, BY COLOR AND RACE

Color and Race	1940	1944	1945-46a	1950
Los Angeles				
Total	1,504,277	1,673,518	1,805,687	1,970,358
Nonwhite	97,847	128,898	---	211,585
Negro	63,774	118,888	133,082	171,209
Other Races	34,073	10,010	---	40,376
San Francisco				
Total	634,536	700,735	827,400	775,357
Nonwhite	31,835	42,280	55,046	81,369
Negro	4,846	17,395	32,001	43,402
Other Races	26,989	24,885	23,045	37,967
Oakland				
Total	302,163	345,345	400,935	384,575
Nonwhite	14,227	---	42,868	55,778
Negro	8,462	21,770	37,327	47,562
Other Races	5,765	---	5,541	8,216
San Diego				
Total	203,341	286,050	362,658	334,387
Nonwhite	6,395	8,100	15,061	18,364
Negro	4,143	7,185	13,136	14,904
Other Races	2,252	915	1,925	3,460

a These figures were taken from special censuses of these cities, each
of which was made on a different date: San Francisco, August 1, 1945;
Oakland, October 9, 1945; Los Angeles, January 28, 1946; San Diego,
February 21, 1946. The figures for other years are the populations
as of April 1 of that year.

Sources: U.S. Bureau of the Census, Seventeenth Census of the United
States, Census of Population: 1950, Vol. II, Characteristics of the
Population, Part 5, 100-03; Population - Characteristics of the Popu-
lation, Series Ca-3, Nos. 2, 3, 5, p. 8; Population - Special Censuses,
Series P-SC, Nos. 97, 109, 173, 188.

TABLE V

TOTAL, NEGRO, AND OTHER RACE POPULATIONS OF
CALIFORNIA AND LOS ANGELES, 1910-50

	1910	1920	1930	1940	1950
CALIFORNIA					
Total	2,377,549	3,426,861	5,677,251	6,907,387	10,586,223
Nonwhite[a]	117,877	162,150	268,991	310,624	671,050
Negro	21,645	38,763	81,048	124,306	462,172
Other Races	96,232	123,387	187,943	186,318	208,878
LOS ANGELES COUNTY					
Total	504,131	936,455	2,208,492	2,785,643	4,151,687
Nonwhite	20,653	41,948	91,586	125,601	273,743
Negro	9,424	18,738	46,425	75,209	217,881
Other Races	11,229	23,210	45,161	50,392	55,862
LOS ANGELES CITY					
Total	319,198	576,673	1,238,048	1,504,277	1,970,358
Nonwhite[a]	13,891	29,809	67,348	97,847	211,505
Negro	7,599	15,579	38,894	63,774	171,209
Other Races	6,292	14,230	28,454	34,073	40,376

[a] Nonwhites are Negroes, Asiatics, and Indians. Mexicans are not included in any "nonwhite" or "Other Race" figures save for the small number of predominantly Indian origin whom the Census classified as Indians.

Sources: U.S. Bureau of the Census, Negro Population, 1890-1915, p. 800; Thirteenth Census of the United States...1910, Vol. II, Population, Reports by the States, pp. 172, 180; Fourteenth Census of United States...1920, Vol. III, Population, Composition and Characteristics of the Population, pp. 106, 114, 118; Fifteenth Census of the United States: 1930, Population, Vol. II, General Report, pp. 52, 69; Sixteenth Census of the United States: 1940, Population, Vol. II, Characteristics of the Population, Part 1, pp. 516-517, 541; Seventeenth Census of the United States, Census of Population: 1950, Vol. II, Characteristics of the Population, Part 5, pp. 57, 84, 100, 163.

complete and composite picture of significant trends in the Black population in the state of California, county of Los Angeles, and the city
of Los Angeles as given in Table V. Of the 175,209 Black citizens
residing in Los Angeles county in 1950, 171,209 lived in the city of
Los Angeles. In other words, except for approximately 11,00 Black
persons, the total Black community was limited to Los Angeles city in
1940. The Black community increased dramatically from 1940 to 1950.
The increase was so noticeable that by 1950, approximately half of the
Black community lived in Los Angeles city. South Central Los Angeles
areas, including Watts, expanded in size. The boundaries were redrawn
to maintain the demarcation between a residential area of Blacks and
Whites.

Watts became a Black ghetto as the population of the South Central
Los Angeles area moved South.[7] In 1940, Watts remained predominately
a middle class district of professional, white collar workers, and
governmental employees. Many restricted covenant cases originated in
the area as Whites attempted to preserve its racial identity.[8] In
1950, the total Black population in South Central Los Angeles rose to
approximately 92,117.[9] Restricted covenants, strictly observed, aggravated housing problems for new Black residents.

The stream of the new Black residents from the rural South taxed
existing transportation and school facilities. The Red Car system,
for example, changed its schedule and routes only when industries that
heretofore refused to hire Blacks relented and cased their employment
policies under these pressures, the Red Car system finally made transportation available from the South Central area.

Once they arrived in Los Angeles, Southern Blacks were forced to
move to South Central Los Angeles or Watts. They could not affort to
pay the higher real estate company prices demanded in the white sections
of Los Angeles. Moreover, because of a high degree of physical visa-
bility, they and Asians found it impossible to escape restrictive
covenants.

Things were different in Watts for the new migrant. Instead of
waking up to the sound of tractors, cotton gins, farm animals, and the
site of rows and rows of cotton, the newly arrived Black, forced to
reside in Watts, woke up to the sound of street cars, automobiles,
police sirens, street vendors, and the site of smoke from industries.
Instead of taking a wagon to the fields to work, one took the Red Car
or walked to work if one had a job. Instead of going trading, one
went shopping. Instead of going to church in the wildwoods, one went
to a storefront church more often than not next door to a liquor store
or pawn shop. Instead of "settling" annually, one was paid weekly,
bimonthly or monthly. Unfamiliar sites, sounds, and new people tended
to disorient the newly arrived resident of Watts and placed him in a
position of isolation.[10]

World War II and its aftermath changed Watts into a lower socio-
economic class community with a heavy preponderance of Black residents.
And it contributed to the economic, political, and social depression
of Watts in other equally profound, yet subtle ways. Many of these

by-products of World War II were at first difficult to detect. One was Executive Order 9066 issued February 19, 1942. This Presidential proclamation formally established relocation camps for Americans of Japanese ancestry. In essence it singled out this group of Americans as the "enemy within" who had to be watched and geographically isolated.[11]

War time xenophobia worked for and against Americans of African descent. It worked for them in that they were no longer the group which received the overwhelming share of White America's hostility. Other groups, including Japanese, Germans, and Italians, were singled out and tacitly charged to prove their worth and loyalty. On the other hand, only Black and Japanese Americans felt a unified national policy of segregation, discrimination and deprivation. The ease of categoration and identification made this largely possible.

America accorded her external enemies many privileges that were denied to many of her citizens. The war policies of the United States contained an infamous duality which strained the foundations of the United States Constitution: Xenophobia and racism. While Americans of African descent felt the full force of this duality before World War II, they now were faced with inconsistent practices such as segregation in the military which made their identity with America seem more precarious.

After arriving in Los Angeles, the Blacks' decision to live in Watts became a matter of economic necessity, personal preference, and an attempt to escape widespread discrimination in housing, employment, and education. For a vast majority of Blacks, settling in the Los Angeles area was tantamount to residing in Watts. Blacks who came to Watts during the 1940's did so in search of more permanent and better paying employment opportunities. Yet the newly-arrived immigrants were unable in most cases to break the poverty cycle.[12]

Suddenly overloaded with a large number of residents confronted with the same problem, Watts was unable to expand services at a rate equal to or greater than the number of people in need. The community found itself unable to deal with the many ramifications of sudden growth: medical care, school curricula, transportation, crime, and housing. What began as individual problems multiplied into social problems which could be traced back to racial discrimination and racial isolation.

The lack of money and jobs followed Watts residents from their point of origin in the South to their final destination in South Central Los Angeles. Of the many variables which contributed to the development and maintenance of poverty in the Watts community between 1940 and 1950, unstable employment ranks very high. A vast majority of the research participants came to Los Angeles seeking employment in defense plants. Their responses indicate employment experiences which were fitful, low-paying, and in some instances, dangerous.[13] They came with few skills and little knowledge of investment or private business procedures. They were unlike the Chinese and Japanese who came with skills in banking, landscaping, manufacturing, and a higher rate of literacy. Unlike Southern Blacks, these earlier racial migrants brought a negotiable core of skills with which to barter with other communities.

The interviews confirm that 173 of the 203 respondents who came to Los Angeles seeking employment found their first job in a defense-related industry. If we add the 32 respondents who indicated that their first job was as a serviceman, we have a total of 205 respondents whose work can be directly attributed to the war. The war, through employment opportunities, influenced nearly 95% of the decision to move into the Watts area. Yet the employment offered by the defense plants was seasonal, low paying, and during the war costly because it was located some distance from Watts. 201 of the participants indicated that their employment lasted only two or three years. 58 participants indicated an initial employment duration of six months to a year, while seven respondents enjoyed the luxury of a job for six months or less. A total of 65 persons in the study were employed for only one year or less. When all three responses are combined, we note that a total of 266 of the respondents worked for only three years or less. The employment record of the participants interviewed sheds additional light on this situation and is graphically explained in Table VI on the next page. Only nine of the 275 participants were employed for four years or longer. Employment was critical for the new Watts residents and the defense industries determined the kind, length, pay, and condition of employment.

Over half of the participants lived with an immediate family which had five to ten members; over one-fourth of the participants lived with an immediate family of ten or more persons. 209 of the participants lived with an immediate family which by today's standards, as well as those of the 1940's, would be labeled large. This point takes on greater significance when it is placed within a context of cost of support. The spouses of 241 of the 275 participants also worked. Even this was not enough, because 89 of the participants lived with an immediate family in which one or more children worked. Despite herculean attempts to break out of the poverty cycle, many failed. They failed, not because of a lack of initiative or motivation, but because steady sources of employment were unavailable even during the war boom.

The figures compiled in Table VI indicates that 171 of the 275 participants came from the states of Louisiana, Oklahoma, and Texas. Of the 171 participants 140 were classified as unskilled. The skills they possessed upon their arrival in Watts were not readily marketable. The participants from the deep South states were also largely unskilled or semi-skilled. By comparison, the figures for Black migrants from the Eastern states show a higher proportion of highly skilled or semi-skilled persons. While the participants from the Eastern states had a proportionately higher number in quality of skills, they nevertheless experienced the same difficulties in finding permanent employment.

The problem of unstable employment was widespread despite the fact that more than one-third of the participants arrived in Los Angeles at

TABLE VI

Employment Record of Interviewees*
(1940-1950)

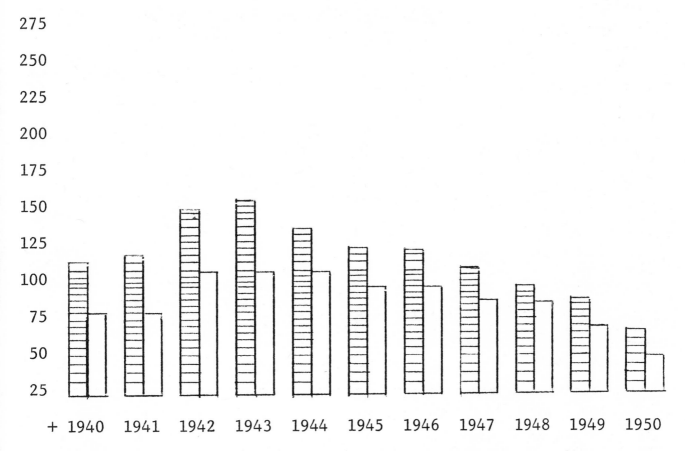

*   275 persons were interviewed (150 women, 125 men).
+   The tinted bar represents employment of female persons interviewed;
    the untinted bar represents employment of males interviewed.

the height of federal defense spending. 197 of the 275 participants came to Watts with a grade school education or less. 55 came with a junior high school equivalent. Only four of the participants had completed twelve years of education.

For newly arrived migrant to Watts, however, education and skills were often seen as of little consequence because of institutional and individual racism.

The story of these migrants is punctuated with miseries inconsistent with the American dream and the level of prosperity enjoyed during the decade of 1940-1950. And as one participant stated during an interview, the final chapter has not and cannot be written until the protagonists (the residents of Watts) and the antagonists (institutional and individual racisms) reach some kind of detente.

TABLE VII

HOME STATE OF IN-MIGRANTS AND LEVELS OF SKILLS

	# of in-migrants	highly skilled	semi-skilled	unskilled
DEEP SOUTH STATES				
Alabama	10	5	2	3
Georgia	9	2	1	6
Mississippi	13	1	1	11
SOUTHWESTERN STATES				
Arkansas	32	3	5	24
Louisiana	73	3	6	64
Oklahoma	41	7	4	30
Texas	57	3	8	46
EASTERN STATES				
Maryland	9	3	4	2
New York	7	3	3	1
Washington, D.C.	13	4	6	3
OTHER STATES	11	5	3	3
TOTALS	275	39	43	193

FOOTNOTES

[1] Judson Howard, "A Picture of Watts in 1913 And of Its Growth Until That Time," unpublished publicity material printed by the Office of City Councilman John S. Gibson (Los Angeles, June, 1973), p. 1.

[2] Ibid., p. 1.

[3] Ibid., p. 2.

[4] Ibid., p. 2.

[5] Ibid., p. 2.

[6] Dorothy Slade Williams, "Ecology of Negro Communities in Los Angeles County: 1940-1959." Unpublished Ph.D. dissertation (Los Angeles, 1961), p. 93.

[7] Ibid., p. 94.

[8] J. Max Bond, "The Negro in Los Angeles," unpublished Ph.D. dissertation (Los Angeles, June, 1936), pp. 28-30.

[9] A Complication of Demographic and Sociological Maps of the Watts Area prepared by The Los Angeles Regional Planning Commission (Los Angeles, 1972).

[10] Op. cit., Dorothy Slade Williams, p. 106.

[11] Lawrence Brooks de Graaf, "Negro Migration to Los Angeles, 1930 to 1950," unpublished Ph.D. dissertation, Department of History (Los Angeles, May, 1962), University of California at Los Angeles, pp. 108-111.

[12] Negro Californians: "Population, Employment, Income, and Education," State of California Department of Industrial Relations (San Francisco, California, June, 1963), pp. 9-11.

[13] Op. cit., Lawrence Brooks de Graaf, p. 18.

CHAPTER 4

THE WAR YEARS AND WATTS: WORKING

Before, during, and immediately after World War II, Black workers
spent a vast majority of their time wearing the label under-employed,
seldom employed or never employed. The search for stable employment
became a very large part of their total existence. One participant
in this study commented:

> ...during the Depression, I spent all day looking
> for work or applying for a WPA job; during the War,
> I spent all day trying to keep my job and trying to
> understand why labor was not as desirable or valu-
> able as the white man's; and after the War, I spent
> a lot of time trying to find a job which had a future
> because I knew that I would be laid off or fired soon.[1]

Another added:

> If you're going to work, you must understand the
> mind of prejudice and I always say what Langston
> Hughes wrote when he stated, "Got one mind for the
> White man to see and another for what I know is me."[2]

Both men emphasized different aspects of the same problem. The
first spoke of the ever-present fear of being laid off and the trauma
of seeking a job. The second concentrated more on the psychological
under-pinnings of this fear and implied that the successful Black job
seeker must understand the White stereotype of the Black worker. Being
able to pierce the psychic of White employers emerged as a recurring
characteristic of each worker who recalled his employment experience
during the war.

The participants who had professional skills conveyed a different
attitude with considerably more anger. They seemed to believe that in
the pre-World War II days successful employment was more a function of
"who you knew" than "what you knew." Table VIII is helpful in providing
information on the employment options and opportunities available to
Blacks living in Los Angeles prior to World War II. The pervasive
variable of discrimination held constant:

> I did not know anyone when I came to Watts; while
> I was able to enjoy a good deal of cultural comrad-
> erie, my cultural comrades were not employed. I
> was left to fend for myself in a job-seeking world
> in which all others seemed hostile, and determined
> to prevent my success in obtaining a job. I came

to Watts in the early 1930's. When I told the
foreman at Long Beach Naval Shipyard that I was
a machinist, he looked at me in total disbelief,
asked me to operate three of his more difficult
machines, and then told me not to let the sun go
down on me in Long Beach. I then took the Red Car
back to Los Angeles City Hall and applied for a
job as a janitor. I retired from my job as a cus-
todial supervisor for the City of Los Angeles five
years ago.[3]

A sense of diminished enthusiasm and self-esteem was quite common
to most of the participants, regardless of their occupations. This is
understandable when we examine Table VIII which indicates the predom-
inant occupations held by Blacks in Los Angeles prior to World War II.

The literature and interviews reveal a frequently omitted fact
of the working world of the Watts resident: on-the-job conditions were
often more hazardous and injurious to Black workers than others.[4]
During World War II, machinery was not only more likely to injure the
hands, arms, legs, and eyes of Black workers, but also the intense
heat, cold, and wind of some job stations lowered their resistance to
respiratory diseases. Professor de Graaf's analysis is supported by
the following statement from a participant:

"This is iron, this is steel, if they don't get
you, the flying debris will?"[5]

The working conditions of Black workers are significantly different from those of their White counterparts because they were not allowed
to join the organized unions which represented their skills. The Black
workers were instead relegated to auxiliary unions. The unions collected and used the dues paid by Black workers without guaranteeing them
the benefits to which they were entitled.[6] This situation was tantamount to "taxation without representation"; or more correctly put,
"taxation with discrimination." Not only did the Black workers frequently fail in his attempt to secure a job for which he was qualified,
but he also, when hired, faced discrimination practiced by his local
union and employer.

Prior to World War II the Watts worker labored primarily in medium
sized industrial plants and retail stores or in the food service area
of hospitals and restaurants. Generally, he was between the ages of
30 and 55, wore a blue collar, and was likely to have acquired between
five and eight years of education. Approximately 95 percent of the
residents interviewed worked outside of their community, because few
jobs were available within the goegraphical boundary of Watts. This
meant that between the hours of 8:00 a.m. and 5:00 p.m., Watts was 90
percent White; and between the hours of 5:00 p.m. and 6:00 a.m., Watts
was 90 percent Black.[7] The Black residents of Watts left their homes
to work outside their community; whites from other areas came in to

TABLE VIII

WORK APPLICATIONS MADE BY 955 PERSONS AT OFFICES OF URBAN
LEAGUE IN LOS ANGELES JANUARY, 1932 TO JUNE, 1932

	J	F	M	A	M	J	Total	Percent
Males applying each month								
Auto repairer	3	--	1	--	--	--	4	0.3
Butcher - Meat carver	1	--	1	--	1	--	3	0.6
Cabinet Maker	1	--	1	--	--	--	2	0.4
Carpenter	2	--	1	2	--	1	6	1.3
Car Washer	--	2	1	4	1	--	8	1.7
Chauffeur	13	9	12	6	5	7	52	11.5
Chauffeur - Butler	9	7	5	2	4	4	31	6.9
Chauffeur - Cook	--	1	4	3	1	--	9	2.0
Chauffeur - Houseman	9	3	3	3	6	5	29	8.4
Cleaner and dyer	1	2	--	--	--	--	3	0.6
Clerk, Bookkeeper, etc.	4	2	2	5	7	10	30	6.7
Cook	4	5	2	1	--	1	13	2.9
Domestic	--	--	--	1	--	1	2	0.4
Electrician	--	--	1	1	--	--	2	0.4
Elevator operator	1	--	1	--	2	--	4	0.8
Laborer	18	14	15	22	11	5	85	18.9
Landscape gardener	--	1	--	--	--	--	1	0.2
Maid or butler	1	1	--	--	--	--	2	0.4
Mechanic	1	2	2	--	--	2	7	1.5
Painter	--	2	--	--	--	1	3	0.6
Plasterer	--	--	1	--	--	--	1	0.2
Porter - Janitor	50	33	21	--	14	17	135	30.0
Pharmacist	--	--	--	1	1	1	3	0.6
Printer	--	--	--	--	1	1	2	0.4
Tailor	--	1	--	1	--	--	2	0.4
Tractor and truck driver	1	1	--	--	1	2	5	0.9
Waiter	3	1	3	1	--	--	8	1.7
Total	122	87	74	53	56	58	450	100.0
Females applying each month								
Clerk, Bookkeeper, etc.	3	5	2	2	1	5	18	3.5
Cook	5	10	3	8	5	3	34	6.8
Domestic	63	48	51	38	30	39	269	53.2
Laborer	21	9	5	8	5	4	52	10.2
Maid	19	9	1	12	15	15	91	18.0
Nurse	11	9	3	1	2	--	26	3.2
Seamstress	3	--	4	1	2	1	11	2.2
Waitress	2	1	4	4	1	2	14	2.8
Total	117	91	73	74	61	69	505	100.0

Bond, J. Max. "The Negro in Los Angeles." Unpublished Dissertation, Department of Sociology, University of Southern California, 1936, p. 174.

claim a disproportionate number of the few jobs which were available.
A Black minister who observed this phenomenon stated:

> To save the souls of my church members, I had to wait
> until the early evening because they are all working
> on jobs in other cities or communities. In fact, at
> high noon, I remember going several blocks before
> seeing someone I recognized. The streets were filled
> with traffic which passed small groups of Black young
> men standing on the corner who were unable to find
> work inside or outside the community.[8]

During the final years of the Depression, a large number of the
participants remained unemployed or had never been employed. Had it
not been for programs run by the Public Works Administration (PWA),
they would not have worked at all. Participants believed that other
emergency jobs programs such as the Civilian Conservation Corps (CCC)
or the Works Progress Administration (WPA) practiced discrimination or
had rules which disqualified them.[9]

More than 56 participants related stories about discriminatory
practicies in the CCC and WPA. Such programs were advertised through
news media often unavailable in the Black community. Lacking information, they also lacked jobs. The information which they did receive,
one participant stated, was incomplete, incorrect or out of date.[10]
When a Black worker was employed by such programs, attempts were made
to make sure that he did not obtain jobs commensurate with his skills.[11]

America's entry into World War II proved somewhat illusory to
Black workers living in Watts. Many participants felt that colored
people were White America's only enemy. They remembered feelings of
bewilderment when the radio described American-Japanese military con-
frontations.[12] They were quite certain about one thing: their battle
for employment, housing, and self-respect had not ended. This was
particularly true in the area of employment. During World War II, the
employment situation for Watts residents underwent little change. "I
couldn't give a damn about the war," one participant recalled,

> "...the Japanese, the Chinese, the Germans, the
> Italians, the Pawnees or White folk of any kind! I
> didn't have a job, I had been out of work for four
> months, my rent was due, my baby was sick and I was
> worried about the late hours my teenage daughter was
> keeping; things hadn't changed for me, whether before
> the war, during the war or after the war. I was
> busted, broke and Black. I didn't care about the
> Army draft, Pearl Harbor, Hitler, Mussolini; I didn't
> care about F.D.R. or his speeches about not having
> anything to fear but fear itself; it didn't mean a
> damn thing to me. I was scared and needed a money
> paying job; you hear me?"[13]

He viewed the entire war as a "ripoff game" with few winners and many losers.[14] Some participants who were not working prior to the war found jobs; still others elevated themselves slightly from the broom or the kitchen to a factory assembly line. Such mobility was difficult and not typical. Blacks had to compete with White housewives, White males who were physically unfit to go to war, and returning veterans. The only competitors who had been eliminated were Japanese. The largest employers of Blacks during World War II were Lockheed, Douglas, Kaiser and Long Beach Shipyards.

Few Blacks interviewed recalled pleasant working conditions during those years. Frequently, they experienced disorientation from the work regime of shifts, and the eight-hour day. They were also unaccustomed to being paid overtime. The wife of one participant explained:

> We came to Watts in 1942 by car from Texas. The
> adjustment or change in environment was hard on us.
> Whereas the entire family used to go to work in the
> fields together, we now worked in different places
> at different times; whereas I used to make one large
> lunch for the entire family, during the war my husband
> and my two sons were able to buy their lunch on the
> job; whereas we used to be paid at the end of the year,
> we were paid every two weeks; whereas we used to be
> paid with groceries or with chickens or pigs, during
> World War II, we were paid by check; whereas we used
> to work from sun up to sun down, during World War II,
> we worked eight hours and were often paid overtime;
> whereas we used to take the baby to the field with us,
> we had to find a babysitter. So you see, our whole
> lives changed when we moved to the city; after a while,
> we didn't seem to be as close somehow. We didn't seem
> to have time to talk. I didn't know what to think when
> my husband came home talking about unions, machines,
> and work shifts. In Texas, I used to churn milk, wash
> our clothes with lye soap, keep our meat in a smoke-
> house and iron our clothes with a flat iron by placing
> it in the fire. During World War II, and now, I use
> an electric iron. We have worked and God has blessed
> us.[15]

Faced with limited employment opportunities during World War II, Blacks in Watts had few dreams about promotions. Paradoxically, they liked and identified with their jobs in many cases, despite wage differentials and white hostility. During this time many recalled a deep sense of patriotism for America, but also bitterness toward America for not providing them with basic rights. They wanted America, but America reluctantly accepted only that part of them which she could use - their labor. Participants told stories about coming to work during the war and finding a monkey or a black cat in their lockers or work area; others expressed concern about staying around after normal working hours. As defense production tapered off, Blacks worked fewer hours in the plants and encountered greater hatred. When defense contracts expired, Black males were the first employees laid off or fired. Their wives, who worked as domestics or for the City of Los Angeles, were not dramatically affected by the end of war production. However, their working experience during the war was not more enjoyable.

Many Black females who worked as domestics prior to and during World War II secured their jobs through church gossip, backyard-conversations, or job agencies such as the Urban League. A domestic could work during the day and come home each evening, or work as a "live-in" and return home only on the weekend. Most women preferred the former situation because they had families of their own. However, some women often chose the latter situation because it provided more food and room for other members of the family.[16]

Some domestics were permitted to bring home bread or rolls, used clothing, and unwanted small household items given them by their employers. Such gifts, especially food items, were very important supplements to the Black families residing in Watts.

Domestics during and immediately after World War II usually earned $5.00 per day. This amount was sometimes augmented with extra money for transportation or "carfare". In some instances, the employer would come to the worker's home to pick her up. The house salary of the domestic worker was also augmented by providing her with two or three meals daily.[17] While the domestic workers did not refuse "extras", they nevertheless felt that their salary could have been higher if it had not become the practice to give away used or unwanted household items. One woman who worked as a domestic noted:

> I never wanted that old, stale, day-old bread that
> Miss Ann gave me, I wanted the money, cash dollars.
> Give me the money and let me go for myself; I didn't
> like that kind of bread anyway, besides it seemed to
> me that she added an extra hour of work with each
> slice of bread. The work was hard and I didn't really
> feel comfortable in an all white neighborhood. The
> only Blacks that I ever saw were the gardener, the
> maid next door, and the garbage collectors.[18]

At the end of the day, the domestic workers of a given neighborhood found themselves standing at the same bus stop, wearing similar uniforms, headed in the same direction: Watts. Some women recalled that they were searched before leaving their employer's home.[19] In addition, they were constantly asked to work harder and faster and frequently threatened with the loss of their jobs if they did not.

Domestic workers were usually required to wash dishes, wash and iron clothes, scrub floors, dust the furniture, make beds, vacuum the carpets, and cook. In some instances they were required to purchase groceries and pick up the children from school. The women interviewed stated that they did not find this work gratifying and fought hard to find other jobs. Few were successful. Once classified as a domestic worker, job placement bureaus would not permit a "transfer" to other jobs, such as elevator operator or receptionist. However, one could become a cook in a restaurant or work in a laundry. The label domestic once applied usually stayed. "I always felt like I was cheating my family," one woman recalled, "because my floors and children were not as clean as Miss Ann's. I liked Miss Ann's free time, and clothing, and always hoped that my daughters would have nice things some day... I tried to get a different job after I got my high school diploma from night school; but everywhere I went they wanted to keep me working as a domestic."[20] Another woman reflected upon her life as a domestic: "I found out that there's a difference between a domestic and a maid. The one way that I could improve myself was going from a domestic to a maid, you see, a maid had more prestige than a domestic worker. It seems very funny now that this is the only career advancement I made. After I became a maid, my work was much nicer because I supervised people and never got my uniform dirty. I was also able to keep nice fingernails and soft hands."[21]

The job turnover among domestic workers was very high because they sought better working conditions, better pay, and locations closer to the Red Car line. The turnover was lower for live-in domestics than for those who came home each day. Live-in domestics tended to have smaller families or no families at all. Normally, a domestic stayed on the same job twelve months.

Although female domestics did not experience a significant shift in their lives because of the war's end, male workers in Watts did. The daughter of one participant reflected upon the impact:

> My father worked in the Long Beach Naval Shipyard
> and I can recall seeing him come home earlier and
> earlier until one day he didn't go to work at all.
> I didn't know what to do because I used to help my
> mother make his breakfast. When I asked my mother
> what had happened to my father's job, she told me
> that my father was tired and needed to rest. I
> really didn't understand until my mother told me
> that she needed some of my babysitting money for
> bus fare. That was a long time age. I was just
> 14-years-old and things are a little better now.[22]

The loss of jobs and the inability to find employment after the war disrupted the plans of many. Participants faced increasing competition and the realization that the number of jobs had diminished sharply. Returning World War II soldiers who demanded the job held prior to entering the armed service, cheap labor from Mexico, and the Japanese all placed the workers of Watts in a precarious situation. For many it appeared as though the circle of job insecurity had come full turn. That is to say, many had gone from the street to the broom or kitchen to the assembly line and were now about to return to the streets. Others, upon returning to the street would think about returning to the South. A wife of one of the participants told how she felt at this time:

> I begged my husband to return to Louisiana because
> we had given the North a chance. It looked good
> for a while, but then all of a sudden the bottom
> fell out. We agreed that at least down South we
> would have a steady job on a cotton plantation,
> with food in our mouths. However, we also realized
> that there were so few opportunities for our child-
> ren down south. We wanted them to get an education
> and be somebody. We already had our chance, and we
> wanted to give them the best possible chance to be
> somebody. I was really scared. We used to go to
> church on Sundays and the minister would tell us to
> hold on and pray. I really thought that we were
> going to return to Louisiana, when we discovered
> how many of our friends felt as we did. Some of
> them did return; we still get letters from some of
> them. They tell us about their jobs down there and
> we tell them about our jobs up here. Of course,
> some of them have moved into cities and are doing
> fine.[23]

After World War II, the road to finding work was long and narrow for the Black workers who resided in Watts. During interviews, several families reported that they saved some money during the War, but the money later had to be used to purchase basic necessities.[24] Three church ministers interviewed reflected upon the serious decline in church donations during the post-war years and a noticeable increase in requests from church members for financial assistance.[25] The ministers also neglected church expenses, such as the gas and light bills, in order to assist needy families.[26]

Not all the residents of Watts were so unfortunate. Some managed to keep their jobs and the returning Black G.I. received assistance from the 52-50 program: $50 for one year.[27] Some participants who served in the Armed Forces recalled that they enlisted because they didn't have a job and found the possibility of sending money back home attractive. Unlike their White counterparts, however, many had no job to claim upon return, even when they came home with different attitudes toward themselves and the world. They returned confused and angry over the inability of their parents and relatives to find employment.[28] Two Black veterans who returned to Watts made the following observation:

> We had just returned to the Long Beach Port and came
> up to 103rd Street and Central Avenue and noticed
> right away the sense of hunger and dismay on the

faces of everyone. Man, the week before we fed tons
of chocolate and spam to people whose names we couldn't
even pronounce; our buddy was killed while spraying
some civilians of Italy for typhus. We looked around
us and couldn't believe what we saw in Watts. We
thought we were overseas again except that all the
faces were Black and many of the names were familiar
and recognizable. We wondered what we had been fighting
for and if we were now going to be asked to save Black
America.29

The families who escaped from Watts during this period tended to
be small. Husband and wife couples without children were among the
first to migrate. They were also individuals who discovered how and
when job information was disseminated and took advantage of such situations. Needless to say, they tended to be better skilled and better
educated. They also tended to be individuals who obtained jobs within
the Watts community such as retail clerks, janitors or handymen. One
such couple in the Baldwin Hills section of Los Angeles recalled not
only their personal feelings of job insecurity, but also their relief
at the realization that money saved during the war went further because
there were fewer mouths to feed and fewer expenses to be paid.30 They
too recalled the reduction in the amount of money raised in church on
Sundays and feelings of discomfort during those days when they returned
to Watts for religious services.

Even during the peak of war-time employment, Blacks encountered
dismal prospects for finding stable employment in the booming Long
Beach and San Pedro Shipyards. They learned that while opportunities
did exist, they had to be fought for because of discriminatory practices in the application procedures.

Those who sought employment at the Long Beach Shipyard had to
initially solve the problem of transportation. The Red Car could be
used only by those who secured a shift during normal day-time hours
of operation. However, most of the participants who worked in the
Long Beach Shipyards during World War II labored between 12:00 a.m.
and 8:00 a.m. If the new Black employee found transportation at midnight, he could usually take the 8:30 a.m. Red Car into South Central
Los Angeles the following morning. His problem was getting there.
Neither bus drivers, taxi drivers, jitney operators, nor private citizens wanted to drive in or out of South Central Los Angeles during
World War II for fear of being robbed, mugged or physically harmed.

Finding transportation from Watts to Long Beach at twelve midnight
was a critical problem. One participant recalled:

In the South, I always knew who was going out of
town and how they were going to get there within
a distance of ten miles around. I would usually
learn of a change in the time at the church on
Sundays. When I got to Los Angeles in 1941, it was

hard for me to adjust to train schedules, I mean the
Red Car, and I didn't like going down to the station
to get scheduling information because the conductors
were prejudice. In the South I felt good riding
into town with a friend on a wagon because one could
talk about our farms and church business. Out here,
people didn't even speak to you when you boarded the
Red Car to go to work. I mean there was just a difference and it took me a long time to get used to it
...to feel good.31

Another participant reflected upon his own transportation difficulties:

I seldom had any money at all and had to count on a
church member or the reverend for transportation to
and from work. I used to go looking for a job with
a friend and when us needed to take the Red Car, we
would buy one ticket. He was very tall and when he
got on the Red Car, he would distract the conductor
and cover the mirror with his hat because he was so
tall and I would sneak on the Red Car through the
back doorway. We were kind of nervous at first, but
we soon got to be good at it, especially if the Red
Car was crowded.32

Still another remembered:

I usually had some kind of job and didn't mind
paying the Red Car fare; but I had real problems
when I got a job at the Long Beach Naval Shipyard
because it took the Red Car a long time to go from
Watts to Long Beach and the damn thing broke down
alot. And when it didn't break down it would have
to wait until the freight train passed. The Red
Car always broke down and rarely got us to work on
time. Man, let me tell you, it was a real hassle!
It was a job getting a job, it was a job keeping a
job, it was a job getting to the job; and I felt
like the White man didn't want me to work so he
could label me lazy.33

Participants reported that they frequently heard about a job
through the NAACP or the Urban League, but were unable to find transportation to and from employment. Most of the semi-skilled and skilled
jobs for which a vast majority of the men qualified were located several
miles away from the Watts area. North American Rockwell, for example,
operated plants approximately fifteen miles east of Watts. Lockheed
was located some twenty-eight miles east of Watts, in the city of Santa
Monica; McDonald Douglas some thirty miles south of Watts in Long Beach;

the Long Beach Naval Shipyard approximately thirty miles south of Watts.

There were no major universities or large governmental offices within a radius of twenty-five miles where the newly arrived Black migrants might find employment as custodians, dishwashers, and laborers.[34] Opportunities for employment in semi-skilled and skilled jobs were limited to local businesses: corner grocery stores, liquor stores, the community garage or auto shop, or night clubs. All but a few of these were owned by whites who did not reside in the area.[35] Those who were fortunate to find transportation outside the Watts area found that their employment options improved. Many found transportation through the formation of car-pools. One participant who worked as an auto mechanic noted that he and some of his relatives bought old cars from the junkyard and restored them for use in car-pools.[36]

Black women in Watts had fewer transportation problems because a majority worked as teachers in local elementary or secondary schools or as live-in domestics in nearby suburban communities such as Westwood, or Beverly Hills. When Black women found employment in the shipyard and aircraft industries, they reported similar problems in finding reliable, inexpensive transportation.

When Blacks applied for jobs at the Long Beach Naval Shipyard, many found the application procedures and requirements ill-defined and unequally applied.[37] They reported going in to apply for a job and being told that there were certain jobs for which Black applicants need not apply.[38] In addition, participants faced the White Defense Unions. They discovered that "Auxiliary Unions" had been established to process the membership of Black applicants and that they were not permitted to join the regular unions in the yards.[39] The experience of one participant is representive of the procedural irregularities encountered:

I didn't know what to expect after I managed to find transportation down to the Long Beach Naval Shipyard. All I wanted was a job and I was ready for anything! I got to the personnel door, lit a cigarette, drank the last bit of my whiskey, took a deep breath and walked into the office. I walked up to the counter and told the man that I was there to apply for a job on the assembly line. He handed me a long application, and told me to take a number from the rack and complete the application while waiting. Now, I had arrived early man, and had number 12. Another Black man had arrived around 10:00 a.m. At approximately 11:45, we were the only ones who had not been waited on from the morning group. The office had waited on everyone else but us. We looked at each other as if to asked ourselves if we were ever going to be called or waited upon. They acted as though they were scared of us or certainly wanted to avoid us. A man came out a few minutes before noon and told us that the office was closed for lunch and that we would have to come back in the afternoon. I was really mad and didn't know if I should shit or go blind! We both went outside and ate the brown bag lunches that we had brought along while sitting on a fire hydrant. At 1:00 p.m., we returned and were told that we would have to complete and pass our physical exam, fill out forms and be cleared for security checks, and provide evidence of having joined the union by noon of the next day if we wanted a job. I really didn't understand the hostility because I thought that we were all American fighting the same enemy. Such requirements were not expected of everyone who applied for a job I later came to know. I had heard some of my friends say that it often took a full week to join the union. Yet we had to do everything in less than twenty-four hours. I wanted to work, the job was available, and I couldn't understand why I couldn't be hired through the same procedure as everyone else.[40]

Other participants described how they felt when they went to apply for a job in the shipyards. "I felt stared at and often thought that I was a fish in a small aquarium trying to avoid the piercing stares of the onlookers."[41] Another stated, "I could not wait until it was time to go home the following morning because I would have an opportunity to talk about the people and how I was treated."

The shipyard workers recalled that some solidarity existed among the Blacks who feared both physical violence from Whites and loss of their jobs. The sense of comradeship was more readily apparent among janitors and assembly line workers than among skilled Blacks who often went out of their way to avoid contact with the unskilled because they felt that such contact would diminish chances for promotion.[42]

Assembly line and unskilled workers agreed that it was possible to recall class differences between the two groups. Only when a Black skilled worker believed that he was about to lose his job, or was about to be demoted did he seek support from his lesser skilled brothers and sisters.

Indeed, this constant threat of job loss and insecurity encouraged community among the Black workers at the Long Beach Naval Shipyard during World War II. This fact, combined with transportation problems forced them into a tightly knit group.[43] They left work at the same time because they feared white violence. One Black female participant recalled "a rash of beatings by Whites at the shipyard during the Fall of 1942; this signaled a warning to Blacks to come and leave in pairs or groups."

Many Blacks who worked at the Long Beach Naval Shipyard during

World War II felt it unwise to work at their maximum level of efficiency; to be innovative; or to produce as much work as their White counterparts for fear of being demoted or moved to a lower job station.[44] In order to keep their jobs, they acquiesced and restricted themselves to mediocrity.

Assembly line workers indicated that they thought of several ways in which to cut down on the amount of time required to produce parts used to make the bulk heads of the battle ships, but kept quiet on this point. Another participant recalled the inordinate amount of effort it took to weld and rivet gun emplacements on the lower decks. He felt that he could have welded twice as fast but did not for fear of what his White co-workers might do or say.[45]

One thing appears certain, the participants who worked at the Naval Shipyard during World War II were highly motivated, energetic, and tolerant employees. Unfortunately, they felt intimidated and threatened.

With few exceptions most participants indicated that their situation changed after they had been on the job for a while and were permitted to work day-time or regular shifts. While there was indication that the atmosphere became more relaxed after a while, each participant interviewed agreed to one point: the kind of job which Blacks were given and permitted to have did not change. There were certain jobs which Blacks could not hold regardless of their background or qualifications.[46] Blacks were not permitted to hold positions of supervision, which required a formal college degree, which required movement to various parts of the shipyards, which tended to provide authority, or encouraged a high degree of visibility. In reality, employment at the Long Beach Naval Shipyard, before and during World War II, turned out to be a major disappointment for the Black migrant in Watts.

The aircraft industry presented similar, if not greater challenges and frustrations, for Black workers because it tended to have few positions for unskilled and semi-skilled laborers. Employment in the aircraft industry, which stood at 30,000 in 1937, soared to more than 2,100,000 at its peak. In 1944 alone, the industry built more than 300,000 aircraft.[47] While Lockheed was the largest of the aircraft firms, others such as the Douglas Corporation built thousands of planes in dozens of plants scattered across the nation from Santa Monica to Chicago.[48]

Hundreds of smaller concerns were also involved. They frequently operated as sub-contractors, producing parts or sub-assemblies of a plane. The implications and opportunities were enormous.

Many old and new residents of Watts attempted to seize the times. They viewed this new industrial giant as still another possible employment frontier and thought of themselves as pioneers or trailblazers. One person who was interviewed recalled:

Man, we were all there the first day. We didn't
know what we were applying for or what kind of

jobs they had; some of us already had jive-time
jobs as porters, janitors or assembly-line workers,
and some of us hadn't worked in months. I had
seen big battleships, but I had never seen a C-2 or
C-4 freighter. Man, I didn't know what a P-38 or a
B-17 was, but I wanted to learn, I wanted an opportunity. When the personnel officer asked me if I
had ever worked on an assembly line or as a techni-
cian to produce a B-17, I was honest and I told him
I didn't know if he were talking about a gun, a
battleship, or a plane.[49]

The aircraft industry established apprenticeship programs, giving
a few Blacks an opportunity often denied them in shipbuilding. To be
sure, white hostility, discrimination, and outright violence toward
Blacks employees existed. However, this new industrial giant did not
suffer the systematic discrimination which engulfed many departments
of the shipping industry. In fact, some Blacks who worked as semi-
skilled laborers in the Long Beach yards, applied for, and in some
instances, were given highly-skilled and technical jobs in the aircraft
industry as mechanics or electrical engineers.

Two characteristics of the aircraft industry (apprenticeship and
new-job classifications)kindled a flame of hope among many Blacks who
sought positions as technicians. This flame was quickly extinguished
by new winds of white racism and budgetary cutbacks as World War II
drew to an end. The aircraft companies allowed a trickle of Blacks
to pass through, but failed to provide them with job security. Moreover, racial prejudice crippled and destroyed apprenticeship programs
and other similar training projects.

During the final years of the War, the few Blacks who were successful in obtaining jobs found themselves demoted to positions which
were essentially non-technical and manual. The dream was deferred as
described by a participant who is still employed by an aircraft industry located in the city of Long Beach:

Deducts and demotions going to be the death of me.
The White boy got the war and all that secrecy. I
talked with my foreman to see what he could do but
he looked kind of strange as if he already knew the
days were getting longer - just like hate and hostility the usual jokes told did not penetrate me,
because the foreman deducts and demotions were an
unholy trinity.[50]

Another participant was less poetic in his recollections. He
recalls:

One day I was well on my way toward becoming an
airline mechanic and the next day I was well on

my way towards becoming a custodian in the tool
shop. In a very short period of time I went from
a position which required expert knowledge in the
use of tools to a position which required only
that I knew how to properly clean and display
them. I felt as if my manhood had been deposed.
I felt cheated or tricked and did not know how
to fight back.[51]

A participant, somewhat more fortunate, remembered yet a different kind of experience.

They let me keep my job as an airline mechanic
but I could tell that I could only go just so far.
I could tell that they did not want me to learn too
much. I talked to some of the other brothers who
worked in the Plant and they said that what I thought
was right because I would not have been in that
position if I was not twice as smart as the White
man. I didn't think that they were wrong because
I used to always show them how to solve a problem.
We all believed that if we were ever going to get
a good job, we would have to be better qualified
and twice as smart as the White man.[52]

Being better qualified and twice as smart was seldom a guarantee
of a technical or skilled position. On balance Blacks found it less
difficult to obtain positions in the aircraft industry than in the
shipping industry, but twice as difficult to keep their jobs. The
salaries for manual labor and for entry level technical positions were
quite similar; the fringe benefits were about the same. However, more
than 60% of those persons interviewed stressed that racial intolerance
was greater in the shipping industry. While some participants believed
that this was due to a lower level of education among whites, others
believe that it was due to the fact that many White employees and
supervisors came from the deep South. Still others pointed to fear
of competition from Blacks, personal insecurity, and feelings that
contact with White women might result in interracial marriages.[53]
Many Blacks who worked in these industries prior to, and during
World War II expressed a willingness to tolerate racial hostility,
discriminatory practices, and the assignment of work-shifts which
were difficult to manage. These individuals were simply glad to have
a job and lacked the desire or emotional strength to protest or organize for protection. In every instance they indicated tolerance of
such practices in order to earn money to support their families. The
following statement was typical:

I went along in order to get along to keep my job.
I dislike what was going on but I disliked losing

my job more. Besides, what could we do anyway?
The man owns everything and runs everything. All
that he does not own outright, he steals. There
was nothing I could do![54]

Another participant recalled:

I was not afraid, but didn't know what to do. I
had no seniority and was still on probation at
work. All of the White people were against us and
we only had a few of us working inside the plant
(aircraft industry). My wife was afraid for me and
would not have been able to earn enough money if I
had lost my job.[55]

A third response is also representative of the concern to earn
money to support the family:

My family was more important than a political fight
or a fight to keep my job. I went in every day (to
the shipyard) and just did my job. I didn't need
another fight because I already had enough. Also,
if I had fought back, I would not have been given
a good recommendation when I tried to get another
job. The man had me going and coming! There was
shit to deal with on the job and shit to deal with
in the streets while looking for a job; so I tried
just to keep my head above the stink and my hands
out of the piles.[56]

The NAACP and the Urban League of Los Angeles made some effort to
organize Black workers during the War years. However, the effort of
these two organizations focused principally upon obtaining jobs, not
improving working conditions or ending White hostility on the job.
The Auxiliary Unions which the Black employees joined were part and
parcel of the Black worker's problems. The Auxiliary Unions for Blacks
took their orders from the regular White unions which in turn often
struck a bargain with employers and management personnel to limit as
well as restrict the hiring and promotions of Blacks in these two
industries.[57]
In summary, the interlude of "prosperity" for Blacks was not
without hardships and severe emotional payment. Blacks endured much
to obtain little despite the hiatus in employment caused by the War.
In the main, Blacks remained poor in the midst of prosperity and fin-
ancially insecure in the midst of bountiful job opportunities. When
one person interviewed recalled being told that the war years were
good years, he responded by saying, "...if things were so good, why
were they so bad." Indeed, things were less than good for the Black
residents of Watts during the war years and rather than diminishing

many of this community's problems, especially employment, have become part and parcel of its maturation into a low-income ghetto.

FOOTNOTES

[1] Oral interview with author, Los Angeles, July, 1973.

[2] Ibid., July, 1973.

[3] Oral interview taken from participant in Los Angeles, June 28, 1973.

[4] Lawrence B. deGraaf, "Negro Migration to Los Angeles 1930-1950" (unpublished Ph.D. dissertation, Department of History, University of California at Los Angeles: May, 1962), pp. 111-120.

[5] Oral interview with author, Watts, June, 1973.

[6] Lawrence B. de Graaf, "Negro Migration to Los Angeles 1930-1950" (unpublished Ph.D. dissertation, Department of History, University of California at Los Angeles: May, 1962), pp. 161-162.

[7] Oral interviews of participants with the writer, Watts, June, 1973.

[8] Oral interview with author, Watts, July, 1973.

[9] Oral interviews with author and several original or older Watts residents who lived in the Black community prior to and during World War II, August, 1973.

[10] Ibid.

[11] Ibid.

[12] Oral interviews with author and several (at least 4-6) participants simultaneously who resided in Watts, July, 1973. It is interesting to note that many participants in the study tended to "open-up" or converse more freely with the author when in the presence of other participants. This is not to say that any one individual was timid when interviewed.

[13] Oral interview with author, Watts, July, 1973.

[14] Ibid.

[15] Oral interview with the author, Los Angeles, August, 1973.

[16] Oral interviews with author, Watts, August, 1973. Many of the participants who worked (some yet work) as domestics during the war years revealed some interesting insights about their jobs and employers;

most of them also shared a common bond as they, too, had families to care for. It is interesting to note that approximately 75% of the domestic participants served as "live-in" help at one time or another. The major reason offered was that it was beneficial to both employee (to have a steady job, food and clothing for their own children) and employer (to be sure of having trustworthy, long-term domestic help).

[17] Oral interviews with author, Los Angeles-Watts, September-October, 1974. According to many participants of this study, the polite "offering of goodies" (food, clothing and household items) definitely influenced many domestics to stay with the one employer longer. It also served to the employer's benefit to have regular or steady help.

[18] Oral interview with author, Watts, September, 1974. This one interview is typical of the many responses or sentiments shared by other domestics interviewed in this study. Working as a domestic was not an easy job; there were many chores to be done (cooking, washing and ironing, scrubbing floors, changing the beds, vacuuming the carpets, and dusting the furniture, along with much other work), and these were expected by the employer to be done daily.

[19] Oral interview with author, Los Angeles, August, 1974. Many of the domestics interviewed rode the same bus or knew of the bus line which took others to and from these jobs. Some of the participants knew one another by name or knew for whom or where one another worked. The fact that some domestics were searched at the end of a day's work primarily indicated that the employee initially had to undergo a probationary period before becoming a regular employee. Today many individuals would view this indignity as exploitation and as a psychological-emotional drain on the employee; however, this practice was the exception rather than the rule and can be argued or interpreted in many ways.

[20] Oral interview with author, Watts, August, 1973. Many of the participants in this study responded or expressed similar attitudes and sentiments.

[21] Oral interview with author, Watts, August, 1973. The participant explained to this writer the difference: "A domestic is an all around woman - she can and is expected to do all kinds of household work." The participant also told the writer it really did not make much difference to the majority of Black domestics in regard to the labels "domestic" or "maid". It was the money and how hard one had to work which made the basic distinction to the Black female "domestics."

[22] Oral interview with the author, Los Angeles, August, 1973.

[23] Oral interview with the author, Los Angeles, August, 1973.

[24] Oral interviews from several female participants with author, Watts, August, 1973.

[25] Oral interviews from three Black clergymen with author, Watts, August, 1973. These interviews were conducted separately with each minister (of different religious faiths) generally reflecting similar opinions.

[26] Oral interview with City Councilman Gilbert C. Lindsey, Los Angeles, August, 1973. Mr. Lindsey is one of three Black City Councilmen represented on the Los Angeles City Council presently. Mr. Lindsey was the first Black City Councilman, elected in 1958, and represents the Ninth City Council District.

[27] Harry S. Truman, The Presidential Memoirs of Harry S. Truman: Years of Trial and Hope, 1946-1952 (1956), pp. 65-69.

[28] Oral interviews taken by author from several World War II Black Veterans, VFW Hall, Los Angeles, August, 1973.

[29] Ibid.

[30] Oral interviews with author, Watts, August, 1973.

[31] Oral interview with author, Los Angeles, August, 1973.

[32] Oral interview with author, Watts, August, 1973. This neatly attired elderly male participant described his occupation to the author and wanted it known that he is now a "retired pimp or hustler."

[33] Oral interview with author, Los Angeles, July, 1973.

[34] Dorothy Slade Williams, "Ecology of Negro Communities in Los Angeles County: 1940-1959" (unpublished Ph.D. dissertation, Department of Sociology, University of Southern California), pp. 84-89.

[35] Oral interviews with author and several participants simultaneously who still reside in Watts, July, 1973.

[36] Ibid.

[37] Oral interviews with the author, Los Angeles and Watts, August-September, 1973. These oral interviews were conducted with Black males who had worked in the defense industries during World War II. Most of these interviews were conducted individually with the author, although some were in groups of five to six participants, yet they generally reflected the same basic sentiments about their experiences in the defense industries.

[38] Ibid.

[39] Ibid.

[40] Oral interview with author, Los Angeles, August, 1973.

[41] Oral interview with author, Watts, August, 1973. The author asked this particular participant to elaborate upon his statement that especially the "onlookers" (referring to white male co-workers who often made jokes about Blacks working in the shipyards) stated angrily and emphatically that "you (the author) don't have the space and place to print my words!" He laughed and the author did too.

[42] Oral interviews with the author, Los Angeles, August-September, 1974. The Black participants who had a skilled job in the defense industries often expressed the views that they were "better (qualified) than the other Black workers," and that they could best retain and advance (econimically) if they did not associate with other Blacks. On the other hand, they were not "accepted as equals" by white peers who had the same skilled jobs.

[43] Oral interviews with author and several former workers in the defense plants, Los Angeles - Watts, August, 1973.

[44] Ibid.

[45] Oral interview with author, Watts, August, 1973. Many Black male participants expressed the sentiment that "too much individual work-production" (output) often resulted in white (males) reacting jealously in the form of sneers, jokes, physical threats, and verbal abuses toward the Blacks. In order for Blacks to keep their jobs, they often "accepted" or "yielded" to these verbal and physical threats by whites.

[46] Oral interviews with author, Watts, September, 1974. Many Black participants pointed out that white prejudice and resentment toward Blacks in the defense industries made it extremely difficult or futile for Blacks to expect job advancements. The FEPC or Executive Order 8802 (June, 1941) issued by President Roosevelt was in fact not enforceable.

[47] Ibid., p. 415.

[48] Warren A. Beck and David A. Williams, California: A History of the Golden State (1972), pp. 414-415.

[49] Oral interview with author, Watts, December, 1974.

[50] Oral interviews with author and several Black participants, Los Angeles-Watts, September, 1974.

[51] Oral interview with author, Watts, September, 1974. This participant expressed very bitter sentiments about his own employment in the aircraft industry, and yet he reflected the general attitudes of the

other participants.

[52] Oral interview with author, Watts, September, 1974.

[53] Oral interviews with author, from several participants simultaneously, Los Angeles, August, 1973. Blacks recalled that they were constantly reminded to "keep their distance" from the white female employees, especially during lunch hours and work-breaks. Blacks interviewed pointed out that their conversations or small-talk with white female employees working on the assembly lines were quite often misconstrued by white males and foremen. The general sentiment expressed by the participants was that they only wanted to work - not mingle with their white counterparts.

[54] Oral interviews with author, Watts, August, 1974.

[55] Ibid.

[56] Ibid.

[57] Oral interviews with author, Los Angeles-Watts, August-September, 1974. See also Lawrence B. de Graaf, "Negro Migration to Los Angeles, 1930-1950" (unpublished Ph.D. dissertation, University of California at Los Angeles, 1962), pp. 270-275.

CHAPTER 5

THE WAR YEARS AND WATTS: LIVING

Housing, like steady work, is very important to individual families and communities. It denotes many things about the overall well being of a given family. More than shelter, it provides the setting for the whole life of the family. Indeed, whether or not organized family life will be possible depends to a large extent upon the character of the house or dwelling unit. Children cannot be reared in a satisfactory manner if there is no place where they can play safely without constantly irritating adults. Over-crowding may drive them out of their homes. This danger may become even more pronounced where there are insufficient recreational facilities in the neighborhood. The presence of boarders, or ghe "doubling-up" of families in a single residence unit, usually means that there cannot be much privacy. Crowding, in general, has similar effects.

In order to understand the fabric of life in Watts during World War II, we shall now turn to a more detailed discussion of the kind and amount of housing available to Black residents.

For Blacks in Watts, housing was a commodity determined by the ever present factor of color. The Black home buyer in nearly every instance paid more for his home or apartment than the White buyer. This "two price" system compounded the ever present problem of unemployment or underemployment.[1] To meet the higher prices, Black families often had to "double-up" or take in boarders, contributing to overcrowding in the neighborhood. In addition, Blacks paid more for martgages, fire insurance, home repairs, and found it extremely difficult to secure credit for the equity in their homes. If they rented, Blacks paid higher rents for lower quality apartments. Often, they found it impossible to find an apartment, or other accommodations short of a house because of the number of children in the family.[2]

White apartment owners used these factors as a convenient excuse for not renting to Blacks.[3] Black apartment owners and property owners in the Watts area took advantage of the situation by restructuring apartment buildings into smaller units to accommodate more renters and increase their profits.[4] While such restructuring did not always comply with building codes, Black property owners seldom worried about these technicalities because building inspections were rarely made in Watts at this time. A Black person, or family, seeking a home or dwelling during World War II, became trapped in a well defined geographical area and paid a price for housing that was at variance with its quality.[5] Both White and Black property owners took advantage of the sudden increase in the demand for housing. On the one hand, White property attempted to contain the Black population; the Black property owners sought to profit from the containment policies.[6]

Because of the increase in the population, housing shortages developed quickly in Watts during World War II. Single dwelling units suddenly became four unit dwellings; four unit dwellings became small apartment dwellings; garages and attics, heretofore neglected, were suddenly deemed fit for human habitation.7 A retired White fireman, stationed in a fire-house near Watts, recalled that:

> ...housing in Watts during and after World War II
> was almost as difficult to find as a building code
> inspector. Newly arrived families in the area used
> to come to the fire station to put them up for the
> night, and we often found men sleeping in the back
> of the fire station during our morning inspections
> ...the material used to build the houses in Watts
> was so poor or had deteriorated because of age,
> that a two bedroom house six blocks away was often
> nearly half consumed in flames before we could
> arrive. The houses were tinder-boxes with unsafe
> lighting fixtures and poor connections for gas
> stoves and other heating appliances. The greatest
> fear we had at this time was the attempt on the
> part of some families to use wood stoves because
> we thought that some sparks from the chimneys might
> set the whole neighborhood afire.8

An employee for the Los Angeles Water Department remembered similar experiences:

> After World War II, I can recall going into some
> houses which had make-shift or no inside plumbing
> facilities at all. When I asked one Black resident
> how they got along, whe replied that she and the
> family went next door. Another resident who had
> no children told me that he and his wife used the
> bathroom before coming from work or in an emergency
> situation used the corner gasoline station.9

Doubling up, tripling up, and the pervasive sharing of appliances and conveniences became common for the Black residents of Watts during this period. Prices were high for everyone but higher for Blacks because they were restricted and confined. The quality of housing was low, but especially low for Blacks because of their greater numbers. Water, gas, and electric service from the city was not reliable: Landlords and city officials ignored calls for assistance; repairmen feared coming into the neighborhood at certain hours.10

Faced with these conditions, many Black families improvised. One participant interviewed came from such a large family that all of the young adult females took "live-in" domestic jobs to make room for the other members of the family. The girls would visit the families on the weekends and return to their jobs on the following Monday mornings.11

If one walked through Watts during and immediately after World War II, the following conditions could have been seen: Original residents occupied the better houses; more families rented than owned a house; garages and attics were used as living accommodations; few homes had larger front or back yards because porches and roofs had been extended to obtain more room; fires were frequent and devastating.[12]

The neighborhoods in Watts at this time were dense and compact. They resembled a large, busy "ant colony" at mid-day. The housing, poor in quality and in amount, was also inappropriate for its occupants. The existing housing was not built for large extended families in which the working members were almost always underemployed and usually unemployed. A vast majority of the dwellings had been built to accommodate small, stable working families or individuals. Few new housing units were built to accommodate the different living or life styles of new in-migrants.[13]

The enforcement of zoning codes was practically non-existent. Warehouses and junkyards sprang up unexpectedly, unplanned, and unapproved.[14] The railroad tracks, built around the turn of the century, expanded within neighborhood streets as though the houses and the children who lived there did not exist at all.[15] This created not only an unsafe condition for men, women and children but also tended to devastate property values. Whether rich or poor, few potential home buyers were interested in property surrounded with noise, unsafe conditions, and human congestion, where alley remained filled with garbage which should have been collected weeks earlier by city sanitation workers. The potential home buyer or renter also had to cope with the problem of rat and roach infestation created by junkyards and warehouses permitted in the area. Few preventive measures were taken by public officials to maintain health standards, despite repeated efforts on the part of community leaders to get them to do so.[16] Perhaps the cleanest and best kept non-government buildings in Watts at this time were the churches.

The post World War II housing problem in the Watts area and its concommitant problem of population density can be graphically illustrated on census tracts. When the area first received Black residents in the 1920's, they were located in tracts 285, 286, and 287.[17] The population later grew to take in tract number 517 as well. The total population of this area in 1940 was 16,955; 5,288 were Black.[18] In 1950, the average number of persons per square mile in the same tracts was 15,922.[19] The total population of the area declined after 1950, due in large part to White residents moving out of the area, the remigration of many Blacks to the South, and somewhat later on, to the expansion of geographic areas, in which Blacks could purchase homes or rent property.[20] These tracts are found at the hub of the Watts community. While the geographical area increased, the large concentration of residents within these tracts changed little. The census map is also helpful in the sense that it permits us to see what is happening to the growth of the Black community in Watts between 1940 - 1950, in relationship to the growth of the Black population in other communities.[21]

Of a total of 577 tracts in Los Angeles County in 1940, 29 contained at least 10% Black residents by that time.[22] Six of the 29 tracts were located outside Los Angeles city. By 1946, each of the 29 tracts had increased their Black population. Also in 1946, the City Planning Commission created 17 tracts in addition to the original 29 tracts. By the end of the year, all 17 newly created tracts housed a Black proportion of 10% or more.[23] This brought the total number of tracts to 45; all of the 17 tracts added in 1946 were in Los Angeles city, by 1950 the number of tracts with at least 10% Black population had increased to 76.[24] At this time only eleven of these tracts were located outside Los Angeles city. The majority of the city's tracts with more than 10% Black population were adjacent to other tracts which already had a high proportion of Black residents.[25]

Only one tract dropped below the 10% level of Black population in 1950. This tract was 446, located in Duarte. The Black population of this tract decreased from 11.5% in 1940 to 3.3% in 1950. Here the Black population was absorbed by an increase in total population from 2,197 in 1940 to 13,267 in 1950.[26] The Temple Street community, bordered by Figueroa, Second, Douglas and Lilac Streets, consisted of census tracts 113 and 115 in 1950, and had an average of 16,666 persons per square mile.[27] The Black population of this area remained rather stable from 1940 to 1950. In 1940, the Black population comprised 2% of the tract's total population, in 1950 2.7% and in 1956 returned to 2%.[28]

In the community known as Little Tokyo, the original Black community in Los Angeles which adjoins the Black Central Avenue community at Pico Boulevard, there was an average of 19,755 persons per square mile in 1950.[29] The proportion of Blacks increased from 4.9% in 1940 to 29.9% in 1950.[30] In the Willowbrook community, which consisted of census tracts 527, 528, 529 in 1950, only five Blacks were listed in tract 529 in that year.[31] The total Black population in this community in 1950 was 16,424.[32] Blacks comprised 47.6% of the total population of the two tracts in which they were concentrated. In 1940, the combined total of Blacks in the three tracts was 1,043. Tract 527 was classified in the consolidation stage in 1950 and tract 528 was in the early consolidation category. Tract 529 had fewer than 250 non-White residents in 1950.[33]

The comparative data given above suggests that once the number and proportion of Blacks in a given area became significantly high, the proportion continued to increase until the area was almost exclusively occupied by Blacks. The expansion of the core of the Black community in all directions to join other Black communities in the city of Los Angeles created an extension of the area occupied by Blacks. This tended to make the Black community in Los Angeles city similar to other Black ghettos such as Harlem in New York City. Although the proportion of Blacks in Black communities continued to increase between 1940-1950, the growth rate showed no consistent pattern.

The growth and expansion of the Black community after World War II did not signal relief from congested and over-crowded conditions

in Watts. As some Blacks began to move or migrate out of Watts, their
space was quickly filled by a new in-migrant, a new birth, or the
destruction of a dwelling which once housed at least one person or
several persons within the same family.[34] Also, little relief was
felt because city officials condemned some of the cheap houses available in Watts by 1950. When Blacks moved outward from Watts, they
complained about having to pay higher rents or prices than Whites as
well as racially restricted covenants. The following statement, taken
from one of the interviews, is illustrative:

> My husband and I, who worked very hard during World
> War II in order to save enough money to buy a descent
> house for our family, were confronted by hostile White
> realtors who tried to discourage us from wanting to
> move into an area recently integrated by Blacks in a
> surrounding community. They refused to take our de-
> posit on a house. The realtors told us that the house
> was already sold and that there were no other houses
> in that area for sale.[35]

Another participant recalled similar experiences:

> We were original residents of Watts who wanted to
> make a change or improvement in our housing situation.
> We had saved our money during the War years and after
> the War, we attempted to buy a home outside the Watts
> community, but could not because of the racial restric-
> tive covenants - indeed White realtors did not want us
> (the Blacks) to expand, they refused to sell us avail-
> able houses once occupied by fleeing White residents
> in the surrounding community. I guess our money wasn't
> good enough for them.[36]

Perhaps the best analysis of the housing problem came from a husband/
wife couple who unsuccessfully took their discrimination case to court:

> We wanted to buy a house in Inglewood. We had the
> necessary amount of money for a down payment, but
> we were told that the house we wanted could not be
> sold to Blacks. We were astounded. We knew about
> the racially restrictive covenants...we decided to
> challenge these damned legalities. We went to sev-
> eral agencies, the NAACP, the Urban League and even
> to the ACLU. Our attorney was a prominent Black
> attorney (Loren Miller). He argued the case in
> court and pointed to the discriminatory practices
> against Blacks in housing in Los Angeles very elo-
> quently. We thought that we would win the case.
> The judge ruled that the racially restrictive

covenants were indeed legal and solely up to the
seller as to whom he wanted to sell his home.
Needless to say, we were deeply disappointed and
worked in the following years to make these laws
illegal by informing other Blacks who wanted to
purchase homes outside the Watts area.[37]

For many Blacks, and many other Americans as well, restrictive
covenants seriously challenged the fundamental ideals upon which this
country was supposedly built. They received little assistance until
the Fair Employment Practice Commission (FEPC), the Rumford Fair
Housing Law (1959), and the Unruh Act attempted to eliminate the
practice in California.[38]

The kind of job which Watts' residents held tended to influence,
if not determine, the kind of housing he was able to secure. Both
factors heavily influenced the type of social life available to a
given family or person in Watts during World War II.

FOOTNOTES

[1] Dorothy Slade Williams, "Ecology of Negro Communities in Los Angeles
County: 1940-1959" (unpublished Ph.D. dissertation, Department of
Sociology, University of Southern California, 1961). pp. 73-113.

[2] Ibid. pp. 113-115.

[3] Ibid. pp. 113-115.

[4] Ibid. pp. 113-115.

[5] Ibid. Also oral interviews with author, Watts, October, 1973.

[6] Oral interviews with author, Los Angeles, August, 1973.

[7] Oral interviews with author, Los Angeles, 1973.

[8] Oral interviews with author, Los Angeles, 1973.

[9] Oral interviews with author, Los Angeles, 1973.

[10] Oral interviews with author, Los Angeles, 1973.

[11] Oral interviews with author, Watts, 1973.

[12] Oral interviews with author, Watts, 1973.

[13] Oral interview with Mr. Morris Ewing, Manager of Jordan Downs
Housing Project in Watts, 1973.

[14] Williams, _op. cit._

[15] Oral interviews of several participants with the author, Watts, September, 1973.

[16] Oral interviews of several participants with the author, Watts, September, 1973.

[17] Williams, _op. cit._ See pp. 84-90.

[18] _Ibid._

[19] _Ibid._

[20] _Ibid._

[21] _Ibid._

[22] _Ibid._

[23] _Ibid._

[24] Williams, _op. cit._

[25] _Ibid._, pp. 134-144.

[26] _Ibid._

[27] _Ibid._

[28] _Ibid._

[29] _Ibid._

[30] _Ibid._, see especially pp. 139-140.

[31] Williams, _op. cit._

[32] _Ibid._

[33] _Ibid._

[34] _Ibid._

[35] Oral interview with author, Compton, August, 1973.

[36] Oral interview with author, Watts, August, 1973.

[37] Oral interview with author, Los Angeles, October, 1973.

[38] Oral interviews with staff members of the Los Angeles Urban League (who wished to remain unidentified) with author, Los Angeles, November, 1973.

CHAPTER 6

THE WAR YEARS AND WATTS: SOCIAL LIFE

With the exception of oral interviews, information on the private social lives of Black residents during the period is limited. These interviews suggest that the church was a very important institution in the lives of the community. With reference to the Black church as a social institution, one participant summarized her experiences:

Many Blacks go to church to see and to be seen.
Indeed, I believe that this is the real reason
why most of them go. If you listen to the conversations of the members, you will find that
the church is a great clearing house for social
gossip. Many members work all the week. Sunday,
at church services, they have the best opportunity
to see all their friends.[1]

Another participant expressed his view in the following way:

I got to go to church. I'm getting out of touch
with things. I haven't heard any news for weeks.[2]

Despite commercialized amusements and social clubs, opportunities for social contacts were restricted. Blacks moved in a limited sphere.

The uncertainty of racial attitudes involved in attending commercialized entertainments was always a deterrent. The Blacks in Watts turned to the church as a social outlet.

The church offered many opportunities to its members for participation in organizations that gave prestige to participants. The Black church during the War years afforded opportunities for normal self-expression and for the development of basic needs - the need for security, recognition, response, dialogue, aid, and new experiences. The church situation provided opportunities for sublimation and offered a medium through which status and some recognition could be gained. Contact with God, as one woman expressed, offered security. As a member of the Deacon's board, choir or ushers' board, the need for recognition could be gratified.[3] An ardent Black church member envisioned the heavenly throne and imagined that he was "on the right side of the Master."[4] Mutual aid among Black church members during World War II was an important part of the regular social and religious program.

Not too distant from church activities, many Blacks during the decade 1940-1950 also engaged in social activities designed for character building and economic relief: The Baptist Teaching Union (BTU) or the Young Men's Christian Association (YMCA).[5] The BTU was a church organization established primarily to offer training to young aspiring church leaders. Young adults who were involved in the BTU taught Summer Bible School during the summer to pre-school youngsters.[6] Also related to the BTU were several week night sessions designed to study and discuss the Sunday School lessons for a given Sunday. Every effort was made to keep the churchgoer in the company of church members. The activities of the YMCA included exposure to Christian beliefs and the maintenance of a healthy body.[7] It was different, however, from the BTU in that the children who participated came from many different Protestant denominations. The YMCA's programs tended to be larger, but suffered because of its orientation toward youth. In the individually sponsored BTU programs, persons of all ages who aspired to be Sunday School teachers learned and worked together.[8]

The social agencies which were oriented toward economic relief, and which served as a social outlet, were the Urban League and the National Association for the Advancement of Colored People (NAACP). In their efforts to promote equal opportunities in housing, employment, education, such organizations frequently sponsored rallies, dinners, dances, spelling-bees and other functions which tended to get the people together while simultaneously promoting and articulating solutions to community problems.[9] The Urban League and the NAACP worked closely with local church ministers; indeed, many of the regional directors of both organizations were themselves ministers.[10] It was sometimes difficult to tell if a local director was speaking for his organization or his church:

> My reverend was very involved during and after
> World War II; I mean he had so many things to do,
> because he helped us 'all' in so many ways. He
> helped my husband fill out his papers for his unem-
> ployment checks; he went downtown to get my son
> out of jail; he helped my neighbor get their son
> put back into school when he had been expelled;
> and he helped us get the children's grandmother
> into the hospital when we didn't have the money.[11]

Another participant spoke of the many roles of the Black clergy in the following manner:

> ...he was a lawyer, a doctor, a teacher and a
> preacher; I mean he did everything. We all needed
> him all the time because the White folk seemed to
> trust and believe him.[12]

Indeed the Black clergy of this day were highly skilled in human relations and served as community factotum. Obviously their community involvement tended to reach adults more than young people. The socio-economic activities tended to attract the Watts resident who was employed, had been in the area some time and was an officer in the church (i.e. deacon, assistant pastor, usher or Sunday School teacher).[13] The umemployed, the less educated or the newly arrived usually bene- fitted from such programs, but rarely participated.[14]

There were, of course, other forms of social life not related to church or social action organizations. During an immediately after World War II, the Watts community developed night club entertainment which combined "Southern Blues" with "Hot Jazz". Such music was called "race music".[15] This was the music of the Honkey Tonk, played loud and with lots of rhythm, it emphasized improvisations and melody. The words often told stories of debts, broken love affairs, loss of jobs, and other similar misfortunes. In the cramped clubs, people also drank alcoholic beverages, played cards, and generally tried to escape the worries of the preceding week. Such scenes could be viewed during week nights but were more prevalent during the weekends.[16] On Saturday night, after days of pent-up frustrations and hostilities, the Black residents in Watts went into the streets seeking ventilation and relief.[17] Homicides, stabbings, shootings, and fist fights were not uncommon.[18] The clubs ranged from small ten stool bars to the corner barber shops which "doubled" as the Saturday night gambling casinos or the large well-organized night clubs.[19] Located throughout the Watts community, the better known and largest social clubs opened along Central Avenue. As unemployment increased near the end of the War, the larger social clubs lost clientele. The community was left with entertainment in the local barber shops or church socials. Some of the smaller places also survived, frequently engaged in unlawful gaming activities, nar- cotics, and prostitution.[20]

The weekend life tended to appeal more to the single, unattached person than to families. However, one did tend to find families and unattached persons involved in church activities and the social gatherings of the Urban League and the NAACP.[21] The large increase of Southern migrants into Watts profoundly affected and, in some instances, determined the social mores. For example, Southern Black women were very accustomed to getting together to make quilts and attending all day Sunday socials during which food was cooked and served for the entire church membership. Southern women also made a habit of visiting the sick and the shut-ins during the week. They took advantage of all these situations to socialize and to catch up on the latest gossip. However, the frequencies of these customs weakened because family ties began, in some instances, to deteriorate. When this happened, many families turned to the church where they found it possible to carry on some of their social customs.[22] During a typical quilt-making evening, the women were able to obtain word of their relatives in the South, news about job prospects, new remedies for colds and other illnesses, as well as news about church romances.[23]

The married men were less organized. They tended to remain at home to supervise the children or listen to the radio.[24] Those who did socialize in groups tended to do so in an impromptu fashion on the front or back porch. Their conversations were full of loud laughter and talk of the neighborhood.[25] Unlike their wives, T-shirt conversations of the men tended to be more entertaining than informative. The married man was able to engage in such conversations while holding the baby on his lap.[26] They talked mostly about sports, women, and their physical prowess. They reminisced about their childhood and swapped stories about discrimination and racism. They compared the South to the North and the White man to the Chinese.[27]

Single, unattached persons, and young adults either participated in church related activities, found solace in local bars, listened to the radio or fantasized.[28] Some formed gospel singing groups which later became leading rhythm and blues groups. Whatever they did, they tended to plan their activities around individuals they had met while working. Their social interests not altogether unlike those of other unattached young persons of the day, tended to be a function of the strength of families, ties and incomes.[29]

What the Black residents of Watts did for recreation and leisure was not always a matter of free choice. They adjusted to and were limited by institutional racism. Sports such as golf, swimming, or tennis, and beach outings were not viewed as viable options because Blacks were unable to find facilities open to them. Just as income determined recreational and housing options, it heavily influenced many other customs and institutions within the Watts community. Income inequality, in turn, prevented the development of an inner economic core and thus brought about the rapid deterioration of the Watts community into a ghetto.

FOOTNOTES

[1] Oral interviews simultaneously with several female participants of this study with the author, Los Angeles, September, 1973. It is interesting to note that many of the female participants were more expressive, and detailed in their attempt to convey a "true picture" of what life for Blacks was like during the decade under study.

[2] Oral interview with the author, Watts, December, 1973.

[3] Oral interview from a Black minister to author, Pasadena, September, 1973.

[4] Oral interview from a participant in this study, (apparently an ardent church member) with the author, Watts, August, 1973.

[5] Oral interviews simultaneously from several participants (who were members of both the NAACP and Urban League) with the author, Los Angeles, August, 1973.

[6] Oral interviews with several participants of this study (who were neighbors during the War and who resided in Watts) with the author, Los Angeles, June, 1973.

7 Oral interview from a Black YMCA employee and participant in this study with the author, Los Angeles, November, 1973.

8 Oral interview with an "original resident" of the Black community (residing in Watts) with the author, Watts, September, 1973.

9 Oral interview from a Black minister with the author. The minister viewed other activities outside the realm of the Church as rather negative influences, Watts, November, 1973.

10 Oral interviews with participants and the author of this study, Watts-Los Angeles, August, 1973.

11 Oral interview from a female participant of this study with the author, Los Angeles, November, 1973.

12 Oral interview with the author (Baldwin Hills), Los Angeles, December, 1973.

13 Oral interviews (with participants) with the author, Los Angeles, August, 1973.

14 Oral interview with several (simultaneously) participants and the author, Watts, August, 1973.

15 Oral interview with the author, Los Angeles, September, 1973. This participant is a retired musician.

16 Oral interview with the author, Los Angeles, September, 1973.

17 Oral interview with the author, Watts, September, 1973.

18 Oral interview from a participant to the author, San Pedro, November, 1973.

19 Oral interviews with several female participants of this study with the author, Watts, September, 1973.

20 Oral interview with a Black retired Los Angeles City Policeman and the author. The participant requested that his name be withheld; this interview was quite brief and the participant's responses and information were quite negative concerning the overall Black community; Los Angeles, June, 1973.

21 Oral interviews from participants (of the local Los Angeles Urban League and NAACP) with the author, Los Angeles, August, 1973.

22 Oral interview from an "original" or older resident of the Black Los Angeles community to the author, Watts, October, 1973.

[23] Oral interviews from several female participants with the author. These participants were also "original residents" (before the mass influx of Blacks during World War II) and ardent churchgoers. They elaborated rather extensively in "recalling the good old days." The Mothers' Board, for the reader, is an "honor distinction" within most Black churches given or placed upon the dedicated and elderly females of the respective churches. Their roles range from guidance, supervision of youths, counseling and assisting or aiding the sick members of the church. Watts-Los Angeles, September, 1973.

[24] Oral interviews from many participants in this study to the author, Watts, July-August, 1973.

[25] Oral interviews from participants to the author of this study, Watts-Los Angeles, May, 1973.

[26] Oral interview with the author, Watts, August, 1973.

[27] Ibid. The participants' comparison of the White man to the Chinese was explained to the writer that both races to them are: "aggressive, very numerous (in population), and devious." The author does not necessarily concur, but for sake of clarity and to illustrate the true sentiments of many of the participants interviewed, the author feels an obligation to convey and report their responses and sentiments; Watts, August, 1973.

[28] Oral interviews from the participants to the author, Watts, August-September, 1973.

[29] Allan H. Spear, Black Chicago: The Making of a Negro Ghetto, 1890-1920 (1970), pp. 147-166.

CHAPTER 7

WATTS: TOWARDS THE FUTURE

From the time they were brought to the shores of North America from Africa and the Caribbean as indentured servants, the vast majority of Black Americans have voluntarily and involuntarily lived in isolated communities with very little control and influence regarding the roles and destinies. They came, most historians have agreed, under dubious circumstances and were forced into living and working conditions which caused considerable disorientation and anguish. Like many of the European immigrants of early colonization days, their status was defined as temporary; however, unlike their European counterparts their status and condition worsened. Black Americans were soon legally defined as chattel or property and later as three-fifths of a human being. Their essential humanity was not recognized until the enactment of the Thirteenth and Fourteenth Amendments. These two amendments permitted Black Americans to be human beings, but were not in themselves sufficient to change their individual and collective psychic as well as that of White Americans. Because of the extremely long period of time during which they were denied their essential humanity, Black Americans had lost all or much of the behavior and attitudes which they brought with them and could only imitate what they saw and believed to be proper human conduct. Until the 1950's, they were constantly reminded of their lesser status through state and local laws and court cases. Black Americans had been given their human status by someone else and their collective identity had been defined by someone else. When Europeans came to North America, their origins were recognized and honored. When a citizen of Italy came ashore, he was recognized as an Italian American. When a citizen of England came ashore, he was recognized as an Anglo-American; when a citizen of Spain came ashore, he was recognized as Spanish American. Thus, these new immigrants were permitted to keep their identity and self-respect. When the citizens from the continent of Africa came ashore, they were called "Colored people," "Negroes," "Niggers," and, of course, the perennial boy. They were not called Afro-Americans.

Only in the past three decades have Black Americans of all political persuasions and all socio-economic levels, successfully set a course for self and group redefinition. There was a time in which many Blacks viewed their ever-present economic plight as solely a function of their own ineptness and lack of intelligence. This is no longer the case. The seemingly unbreakable cycle of poverty and ghetto life has many stages which are perpetuated through both internal and external factors. While the mixture of the forces is not necessarily balanced or equal in impact, they do nevertheless exist. To redefine self is tantamount to redefining those forces which influence one's universe; to redefine self is tantamount to looking at one's universe with fresh eyes, eyes which had not been used previously.

While not all Blacks have moved toward group-redefinition, a sufficient number have identified with it to suggest that Black or Afro-American is a highly preferable identity than Negro.

That the Black community has worked for group-redefinition and has made important strides toward gaining control over those forces which guide its destiny, is a fact which few, if any, historians will question. Their success in this area has greatly increased their alternatives for the future. Not long ago the conventional wisdom about the future of the Black community was unilaterally bleak and pessimistic. However, since the sit-ins, demonstrations, court decisions, changes in the attitudes and behavior of White Americans, and the election of a large number of Black public officials, the alternatives for the Black community have improved in number and quality. We have discussed the maturing of one Black community. The future of Black communities such as Watts is inextricably bound to the future of America.

We can hypothesize some possible futures for Black communities such as Watts. In his article, "Alternative Futures for the American Ghettos," Professor Anthony Downs presents what he believes to be basic alternatives relevant to ghettos.[1] In outline form, they are:

1. The Present-Policy Strategy. He notes that..."in order to carry out this strategy, we need merely do nothing more than we do now. Even existing federal programs aimed at aiding cities - such as the Model Cities Program - will continue or accelerate concentration, segregation, and non-enrichment, unless those programs are colosally expanded...the strategy of continuing our present policies and our present level of effort is essentially not going to alter current conditions in ghettos."

2. The Enrichment-Only Strategy. He notes that... "the basic idea underlying the enrichment-only strategy (and part of every other strategy involving enrichment) is to develop federally financed programs that would greatly improve the education, housing, incomes, employment and job-training, and social services received by ghetto residents. This would involve vastly expanding the scale of present programs, changing the nature of many of them because they are now ineffective or would be if operated at a much larger scale, and creating incentives for a much greater participation of private capital in ghetto activities.

3. The Integrated-Core Strategy. He notes that... "This strategy is similar to the enrichment-only strategy because both would attempt to upgrade the

quality of life in central-city ghettos through
massive federally assisted programs. The integrated-core strategy would also seek, however, to
eliminate racial segregation in an ever expanding
core of the city by creating a socially, economi-
cally, and racially integrated community there.
This integrated-core would be built up through
large-scale urban renewal programs, with the land
re-uses including scattered-site public housing,
middle-income housing suitable for families with
children, and high-quality public services -
especially schools."

4. The Concepts of Dispersal. He notes that
"...the two dispersal strategies concerning the
future of ghettos are both based upon a single key
assumption: that the problems of ghettos cannot
be solved so long as millions of Blacks, particularly those with low income and significant disad-
vantages, are required or persuaded to live together
in segregated ghetto areas within our central cities.
These strategies contend that large numbers of Blacks
should be given strong incentive to move voluntarily
from central cities into suburban areas, including
those in which no Blacks presently reside."

The last concept would represent a radical change in existing
trends. Not only would it stop expansion of Black ghettos in central
cities, but it would also inject a significant Black population into
many presently all-White suburban areas. Such policies would represent a marked departure from past American practice. A sharp break
with the past would be necessary for any significant dispersal of
Blacks. Merely providing the opportunity for Blacks to move out of
ghettos would, at least in the short run, not result in much change.
Even adoption of a vigorously-enforced nationwide open-occupancy law
would not greatly speed up the present snail's pace rate of dispersion.
Income inequality remains a more powerful barrier than law.
    Other scholars, of course, hypothesize different futures for
Black communities such as Watts. Professor Robert S. Brown of Fair-
leigh Dickinson University advocates economic Black power as the only
real viable future for the Black community; Robert S. Lockey and H.
Elliot Wright maintain that the Black community should embark upon a
program of reparation in a fashion similar to the Jews after World
War II. The Black Muslims advocate a program of self-help and volun-
tary separation; and the NAACP and the Urban League advocate a rather
complex program of close partnership with the Federal Government and
the Courts. More recently the Symbionese Liberation Army presented
an alternative which suggests massive military physical force. The
programs composed by each of these groups are in part a consequence

of their perspectives on the present and the future status of Black community.

In my view, the future status of Watts may take three possible directions. The first is massive out-migration of those residents who arrived prior to and during World War II, as well as those who have arrived since the 1965 rebellion. The out-migration could be so massive as to change the area into a ghost town. This alternative future is particularly noteworthy because of the high unemployment rate which such communities such as Watts has been known to reach levels as high as 35% to 40%. When this happens, there is a noticeable change in the number of out-migrants. Conventional wisdom in Watts has it that there is already underway an exodus back to the South. If this is true, one might ask if this will mean more jobs available for those who are left? In point of fact, the number of jobs available is declining faster than the rate of out-migration. Equally important is the fact that the jobs which are left tend to be either menial, low-wage jobs or require skills which are not found within the Watts labor force. A ghost town then, or less pessimistically, a decline in population density is a likely alternative direction for the Watts community.

On the other hand, Watts could become an industrial park area. This possibility is especially imminent in view of its proximity to the Compton-Wilmington Industrial Park area and the City of Vernon, known as the City of Industry. Additionally, Bethlehem Steel Company, a large manufacturing plant, occupies nearly two miles from 103rd Street and Alameda to the Firestone Rubber Plant on the corner of Alameda and East Firestone Boulevard. Other industrial facilities now in the Watts area include railroad tracks which criss-cross the entire community, junkyards, and small steel melting plants which dot Alameda Boulevard. All of these characteristics of the area can be quickly and inexpensively developed. Once this is done, the area would easily compliment surrounding communities. The change or development of this area into an industrial part would be for small industries only and would definitely affect every aspect of community life. The Watts Manufacturing Company on El Segundo Boulevard, the Shanda Toy Manufacturing Company on Central Avenue, the various enterprises of the Watts Community Labor Action Council, and the various other small Black owned industries in the area could serve as a foundation if this option were to be seriously considered in the future by local and national officials.

A third possible alternative future for Watts community is that the area and its people could become victims of urban renewal. This possibility can be easily illustrated by viewing the major metropolitan areas of the East and Midwest, (Washington, D.C., New York, St. Louis, Chicago, and others), where Blacks living in deteriorated slum conditions became victims of urban renewal programs and exorbant rent which they could not afford. This alternative future is possible for the Watts area, especially if the urban renewal project involved the erection of a large government complex such as a new office for the Veterans Administration, Health, Education and Welfare, and Housing.

Employees of such large government complex would seek housing as close to their jobs as possible. A similar phenomenon can be presently seen in the Los Angeles downtown area following the erection of Bunker Hills Towers. These very expensive living accommodations were built to satisfy the housing needs of the employees of the World Trade Center, The Richfield Plaza, and the downtown business area. Even if low-cost housing were a part of the new facilities, it would be out of reach for the original Black residents. Low-income blue collar residents would be displaced by middle-class white collar residents; urban renewal would become a program for Black removal.

In sum, Watts is more people than land or a cluster of buildings. The forces which will determine the future of Watts are external to it, just as it has become increasingly apparent that global interdependence is the overriding characteristic of World affairs; so too is it apparent that community interdependence is the overriding character of contemporary life in America. The significance of this fact has not yet reached full potential but will certainly be manifested in future problem solving efforts. Thus one cannot talk about the future of Watts without talking about the future of California and America. Because this community is not an isolated community capsule it will, no doubt, be necessarily affected by events in which it had no role in making.

This author believes that one thing is obvious: the recent sudden decline in the standard of living in America generally has affected the standard of living in California which in turn has affected the standard of living in Watts. As prices for all products in the country rise, there is a corresponding or greater rise in prices for products in Watts; as unemployment figures rise in the country, there is a corresponding or greater rise in unemployment in Watts. The golden age of prosperity in America has ended for everyone and will not likely return in the dimensions of the recent past. If the Black residents of Watts have been poor in the past, many of them will continue to be so categorized in the future. Some will be successful in their struggle for recategorization; however, they will be the exception rather than the rule. What is suggested here is that there is an obvious symbiotic relationship between smaller community entities such as Watts, and larger community entities such as the city of Los Angeles, the county of Los Angeles or the State of California. The ability of major economic and social policy makers to develop and maintain viable links between those larger and smaller community entities will not only determine how well a given one will improve, but also whether or not all of them will survive. For the future, the need and watchword will be interdependence.

The future of Watts then will be largely determined by the future of America. It may be a future marked by hope and reconstruction, or gradual decay and a perpetuation of a dual society: One Black, one White; separate and unequal.

FOOTNOTE

[1] Anthony Downs, "Alternative Futures for the American Ghetto," <u>The Enduring Ghetto</u>, David R. Goldfield and James B. Lane (1973), pp. 233-245.

CHAPTER 8

NOTES ON METHODOLOGY

The basic underlying purpose of this study was to analyze the role played by World War II in the development of Watts as a Black ghetto. A secondary purpose was to examine the economic and social life of Watts residents, who came to the area from the South during the decade of 1940-1950. This study used oral history as a basic tool of research.

The great amount of sociological and historical data has been gathered on the South Central Los Angeles area, particularly since the Watts rebellion of 1965: the McCone Commission report, published in 1966, and the work of Professor Lawrence Brooks de Graaf. However, neither of these large efforts, nor many of the smaller ones, attempted to determine how, why, and through what process Watts changed from a middle class community of Whites, Mexican-Americans, and various other ethnic groups to a lower class, predominately Black ghetto.

By means of oral interviews, I collected verbal accounts of significant events from individuals who participated in them or who were close to someone who had first hand knowledge of the incidents. The technique used was the network system. To construct the network system, I spent considerable time in the Watts area in an effort to locate individuals who had come from the South prior to or during the decade of 1940-1950, and who remained. The second type of person who was sought out was a resident who knew someone who had come to the area prior to or during the same time period. Through the network system then, an effort was made to discover a pattern of social relationships among friends, neighbors, and relatives living in the area and the interactions of these groups. Great difficulty was experienced in finding families and individuals. As I expected, many families or individuals were unwilling to participate in the research project because the area has been bombarded with other poll-takers, opinion surveyors and college graduate students. The issue of individual privacy was also involved. Extreme care was taken when preparing each item in the questionnaire to make certain that it was clear, concise, and communicated the desired meaning. Questions which were possibly embarassing were omitted.

The questionnaire was divided into two parts. The first part was designed to gather data on the decision to migrate to Los Angeles and the encounters of the trip to Los Angeles; the second part was designed to gather data after arrival. I attempted to keep both parts of the questionnaire as short as possible in order to avoid fatigue and redundancy. Qualified residents were located through community churches, the local Social Security Office, City Council Offices, representing the geographical area, the Los Angeles City and County Commission on Human Relations and the Welfare Offices. Doctors, lawyers and other professionals who practiced in the area ten years or more were contacted. Once a small group of qualified residents were identified, it was relatively easy to locate others as the network snowballed. A total of 478 oral interviews were conducted and completely by the author. However, only 275 oral interviews and responses to the questionnaires could be utilized in this study because this was the total which met all the inclusive criteria necessary to complete the research.

Three basic stages were involved in the information-gathering process. In the first stage, I attempted to learn about the community and to build up a level of trust between residents and myself. Accompanied by formal letters of introduction, intent and purpose of the research (written in behalf of this author by his Ph.D. Chairman, Dr. Michael E. Parrish) to various Black and White Los Angeles community leaders, I became involved - interacted and collected data throughout the Black community. Councilmen Billy G. Mills and Gilbert C. Lindsey were particularly helpful as was Ellis P. Murphy, Director of the Los Angeles County Department of Social Services. Theordore Watson, Director of the Watts Labor Action Council, along with other influential Black Los Angeles leaders, provided some contacts and assistance. Each oral interview lasted approximately sixty to ninety minutes.

The second stage of the information-gathering process involved recording the information given by the participants. Nearly all interviews were conducted with a tape recorder. Before leaving each person interviewed, the tape was played back to give him or her an opportunity to make any corrections or add to the information given. For those interviews conducted without a tape recorder, a summary was provided for the participant to check for thoroughness. The third stage of the information-gathering process was analyzing and interpreting the data. I listened to the tape recordings more than once to make certain that all salient points of information came through. The written questionnaires were thoroughly reviewed by the author and categorized.

In determining the procedures to be used in collecting the data and developing the network system, the author relied heavily upon the methodology of the network system outlined by Professors Elizabeth Bott and Aaron Victor Cicourel. Professor Bott's description of the network system is found in Family and Social Network - Roles, Norms, and External Relationships in Ordinary Urban Families; Professor Cicourel's statements and description of the network system is found in Method and Measurement in Sociology. Their works became instrumental in forming the guidelines given above. The network system may be defined as an examination of the relationship between families and society and the manner in which families and individuals interact with external persons and institutions. Additionally, the aim of the network system is to understand and penetrate the social organizations and patterns of behavior of some urban families. It is a pattern of social relationships with and among friends, neighbors, and relatives. Needless to say, the techniques used by the interviewer or investigator play a crucial role in the data obtained.

BIBLIOGRAPHY

Oral Interviews. There were 478 oral interviews conducted by the
    author with the participants of this study. Of the 478 oral
    interviews, conducted between June, 1973, and January, 1975,
    only 275 participants met all the criteria to complete the
    questionnaires. The oral interviews were conducted in the Los
    Angeles area, especially among the Watts residents. The majority
    of those who did not meet the criteria fall into four major cate-
    gories: (1) could not recall; (2) resided in Watts or Los Angeles
    only a certain number of years; (3) did not want to reveal any
    more information; and (4) had no more extra time. All of the oral
    interviews remained anonymous to the reader, with the exception
    of those public officials and Black community leaders who did not
    mind publicly revealing their names or addresses.

Abrams, Charles. "The Housing Problem and the Negro." Daedalus
    (Winter 1966), pp. 64-66.

Aldrich, Howard E. "Employment Opportunities for Blacks in the Black
    Ghetto: The Role of White-Owned Business." The American Journal
    of Sociology, 78 (May 1973), pp. 1403-25.

Allen, Robert. Black Awakening in Capitalist America: An Analytic
    History. New York, New York, Doubleday, 1969.

American Civil Liberties Union, "Police Malpractice and the Watts
    Riots" (1966).

American Civil Liberties Union, "Police Power vs. Citizens' Rights:
    The Case for an Independent Police Review Board" (1966).

Annual Publications of the Historical Society of Southern California.
    Commemorating the One Hundred and Fiftieth Anniversary of the
    Founding of Los Angeles, September 4, 1781. New York, New York,
    The McBride Printing Company, 1931.

Badikan, Ben. H., In the Midst of Plenty: The Poor in America.
    Boston, Beacon Press, 1964.

Bancroft, Hubert Howe. History of California. Vol. I: 1542-1800.
    San Francisco, A.L. Bancroft and Company, 1884.

Banfield, Edward. Big City Politics. New York, New York, Random
    House, 1965.

Beasley, Delilah L. The Negro Trail Blazers of California. Los Angeles, 1919, 317 pp.

_____. Essentials of Americanization. Los Angeles, The Jesse Ray Miller Company.

_____. Fundamentals of Social Psychology. New York, New York, The Century Company, 1924, 479 pp.

_____. The New Social Research. Los Angeles, The Jesse Ray Miller Company, 1926, 287 pp.

Bell, Carolyn. The Economics of the Ghetto. New York, New York, Pegasus Company, 1970.

Bendix, Richard and Seymour Lipset (eds.). Class, Status and Power. Glencoe, Illinois, The Free Press, 1953.

Bennett, Elain E. Calendar of Negro-Related Documents in the Records of the Committee for Congested Production Areas in the National Archives. Washington, American Council of Learned Societies, 1949.

Bennett, Lerone. Before the Mayflower, 4th ed. Chicago, Illinois, Johnson Publishing Company, 1969.

_____. "Liberation." Ebony, 25 (1970), pp. 36-45.

_____. "The Making of Black America: The Black Worker, Part X." Ebony, 27 (December 1972), pp. 73-79, and (November 1972), pp. 118-122.

Berger, Bennett M. Working-Class Suburb. Berkeley, California, University of California Press, 1969.

Bicknell, Marguerite E. and Margaret C. McCulloch. Guide to Information About the Negro and Negro-White Adjustment. Memphis, Tennessee, Brunner Publishing Company, 1943.

Bigger, Richard and James D. Kitchen. How the Cities Grew. Los Angeles, California, The Haynes Foundation, 1952.

"The Black Revolution." Ebony, 24 (August, 1969).

Blackwell, James E. and Marie Haug. "Relations Between Black Bosses and Black Workers." The Black Scholar, 4 (January 1973), pp. 36-43.

Blalock, Hubert M. "A Power Analysis of Racial Discrimination." Social Forces, 39 (1960), pp. 53-69.

_____. _Toward A Theory of Minority-Group Relations_. New York, New York, Capricorn Books, 1967.

Blauner, Robert. "Internal Colonialism and Ghetto Revolt," _Social Problems_, Spring 1969, pp. 393-408.

_____. "Whitewash Over Watts," _Transaction_, III (1966), pp. 3-9.

Blaustein, Albert P. and Robert L. Zangrando (eds.), _Civil Rights and the American Negro_. New York, New York, Washington Square Press, Inc., 1968.

Blumberg, Leonard. _Migration As a Program Area for Urban Social Work: A Pilot Study of Recent Negro Migrants into Philadelphia_. Philadelphia, Pennsylvania, Urban League of Philadelphia, 1958.

Bogue, Donald J. _The Population of the United States_. Glencoe, Illinois, Free Press, 1959.

_____. "Urbanism in the United States, 1950," _American Journal of Sociology_, LX (March, 1955), pp. 471-484.

Bond, J. Max. "The Negro in Los Angeles." (Unpublished dissertation for the University of Southern California, 1936).

Bontemps, Arna and Jack Conroy. _They Seek a City_. Garden City, New Jersey, Doubleday, Doran and Company, 1964.

Bott, Elizabeth, _Family and Social Network_. London, England, Tavistock Publications Limited, 1964.

Bracey, John H., August Meier and Elliott Rudwick (eds.). _Black Nationalism in America_. Indianapolis, Indiana, Bobbs-Merrill, 1970.

_____. _The Rise of the Ghetto_. Belmont, California, Wadsworth Publishing Company, 1971.

Branyan, Robert L. and Lawrence H. Larsen (eds.). _Urban Crisis in Modern America_. Lexington, Massachusetts, D.C. Heath and Company, 1971.

Buell, R.L. "The Development of Anti-Japanese Agitation in the U.S.A." _The Political Science Quarterly_, XXXVIII (March 1933), pp. 57-81.

Burnight, Ralph F. _The Japanese in Rural Los Angeles County_. Studies in Sociology, Sociological Monograph, No. 16. Los Angeles, University of Southern California, June, 1920.

Callow, Alexander S., Jr. (ed.). <u>American Urban History</u>. New York, New York, Oxford University Press, 1969.

Carmichael, Stokely and Charles V. Hamilton. <u>Black Power: The Politics of Liberation in America</u>. New York, New York, Random House, 1967.

Cayton, Horace M. and St. Clair Drake. <u>Black Metropolis: A Study of Negro Life in a Northern City</u>. New York, New York, Harper and Row, 1945.

Cayton, Horace M. and George S. Mitchell. <u>Black Workers and the New Unions</u>. Chapel Hill, North Carolina, The University of North Carolina Press, 1939.

Chapman, Charles E. <u>A History of California: Spanish Period</u>. New York, New York, The Macmillan Company, 1921.

Cicourel, Aaron V. <u>Method and Measurement in Sociology</u>. New York, New York, Free Press of Glencoe, 1964.

Clark, Kenneth B. <u>Dark Ghetto: Dilemmas of Social Power</u> (New York, 1965).

Cohen, Jerry and William S. Murphy. <u>Burn, Baby, Burn! The Los Angeles Riot: August 1965</u> (New York, 1966).

Collins, Henry Hill, Jr. <u>America's Own Refugees: Our 4,000,000 Homeless Migrants</u>. Princeton, New Jersey, Princeton University Press, 1941.

Connery, Robert H. (ed.). <u>Urban Riots, Violence and Social Change</u>. New York, New York, Vintage Books, 1969.

Conot, Robert. <u>Rivers of Blood, Years of Darkness</u>. (New York, 1967).

Crump, Spencer. <u>Black Riot in Los Angeles</u> (Los Angeles, 1966).

Cruse, Harold. <u>The Crisis of the Negro Intellectual</u>. New York, New York, William Morrow, 1967.

Dees, Jesse Walter, Jr., and James S. Hadley. <u>Jim Crow</u>. Ann Arbor, Michigan, Ann Arbor Publishers, 1951.

Donald, Henderson H. <u>The Negro Freedman</u>. New York, New York, Henry Schuman, 1952.

_____. "The Negro Migration of 1916-1918," <u>The Journal of Negro History</u>, VI (October, 1921), pp. 383-498.

Drake, St. Clair. "The Social and Economic Status of the Negro in the United States," Daedalus, XCIV (Fall 1965), pp. 771-814.

Drake, St. Clair and Horace R. Cayton. Black Metropolis. New York, New York, Harcourt, Brace and Company, 1945.

Draper, Harold. Jim Crow in Los Angeles. Los Angeles, California, Worker's Party, 1946.

DuBois, W.E.B. "The Black North: A Social Study," New York Times (November 17, 1901 - December 15, 1901).

Dunaway, Clyde A. "Report of the Proceedings of the Pacific Coast Branch." Annual Report of the American Historical Association for the Year 1907. Washington, D.C., The Government Printing Office, 1908, Vol. I, 38 pp.

Eaves, Lucille. A History of California Labor Legislation. The University of California Publications in Economics, Vol. II, Berkeley, California, The University Press, 1910.

Edwards, Paul K. The Southern Urban Negro as a Consumer. New York, New York, Prentice-Hall, Inc., 1932, 323 pp.

Fogelson, Robert M. The Fragmented Metropolis: Los Angeles, 1850-1930 (Cambridge, Massachusetts, 1967).

_____. Violence As Protest. Garden City, New York, Doubleday and Company, Inc., 1971.

_____. "White on Black: A Critique of the McCone Commission Report on the Los Angeles Riots," Political Science Quarterly, September 1967, p. 342.

Fogelson, Robert M. and Robert E. Hill, "Who Riots? A Study of Participation in the 1967 Riots, Supplemental Studies for the National Advisory Commission on Civil Disorders, Washington, D.C., Government Printing Office, 1968.

Foner, Eric. "In Search of Black History." New York Review of Books, October 22, 1970, pp. 11-14.

Forman, Robert E. Black Ghettos, White Ghettos, and Slums. Englewood Cliffs, New Jersey, Prentice-Hall, 1971, p. 78.

Franklin, John Hope. From Slavery to Freedom. New York, New York, Alfred A. Knopf, 1948.

Franklin, John Hope and Isidore Starr (eds.). The Negro in 20th Century America. New York, New York, Vintage Books, 1967.

Frazier, E. Franklin. "Occupational Classes Among Negroes in Cities." The American Journal of Sociology, XXXV (March 1930), pp. 713-730.

_____. The Black Bourgeoisie (New York, 1962).

_____. The Negro Family in Chicago. Chicago, Illinois, University of Chicago Press, 1932.

_____. The Negro Family in the United States, Chicago, Illinois, University of Chicago Press, 1939.

_____. The Negro Family in the United States, rev. ed. Chicago, Illinois, University of Chicago Press, 1966.

"Geographical Variations in Hours and Wages During 1933 and 1935," Monthly Labor Review, XLVII (July, 1938), pp. 117-145.

Geschwender, James A. "Social Structure and the Negro Revolt: An Examination of Some Hypotheses." Social Forces.

Gillin, John Lewis, Poverty and Dependency, Their Relief and Prevention. New York, New York, The Century Company, 1921, 707 pp.

Glaab, Charles N. and A. Theordore Brown. A History of Urban America. Toronto, Ontario, the Macmillan Company, 1967.

Glazer, Nathan and Davis McEntire (eds.). Studies in Housing and Minority Groups. Berkeley, California, University of California Press, 1960.

Glazer, Nathan and Daniel P. Moynihan. Beyond the Melting Pot. Cambridge, Massachusetts, the M.I.T. Press, 1963.

Goldfield, David R. and James B. Lane. The Enduring Ghetto. Philadephia, Pennsylvania, J.B. Lippincott and Company, 1973.

Goodrich, Carter et al. Migration and Economic Opportunity. Philadelphia, Pennsylvania, University of Pennsylvania Press, 1936.

Gordon, Margaret. Employment Expansion and Economic Growth, The California Experience: 1900-1950. Berkeley, California, University of California Press, 1954.

de Graaf, Lawrence Brooks. "Negro Migration to Los Angeles, 1930 to 1950." (unpublished dissertation for the University of California at Los Angeles, 1962.)

Granger, Lester B.   "Negroes and War Production," Survey Graphic,
    XXXI (November, 1942), pp. 469-471, 543-544.

Grigsby, William G.   Housing Markets and Public Policy.   Philadelphia,
    Pennsylvania, University of Pennsylvania Press, 1963, Chapter 8.

Grodzins, Morton.   The Metropolitan Area as a Racial Problem.
    Pittsburgh, Pennsylvania, University of Pittsburgh Press, 1959.

de Groot, Adrian D.   Methodology.   The Hague, Paris, France, Mouton
    and Company, 1969.

Groves, Ernest R.   An Introduction to Sociology.   New York, New York,
    Longmans, Green and Company, 1928.

Gulick, Sidney L.   Evolution of the Japanese.   New York, New York,
    F.H. Revell Company, 1903.

Handlin, Oscar.   Boston's Immigrants.   Cambridge, Massachusetts, 1959,
    pp. 186-190.

_____.   "The Modern City as a Field of Historical Study," The
    Historian and the City, ed.   Oscar Handlin and John Burchard.
    Cambridge, Massachusetts, M.I.T.   Press and Harvard University
    Press, 1963, p. 25.

_____.   The Uprooted.   Boston, Massachusetts, Little, Brown and
    Company, 1952.

Harrington, Michael.   The Other America: Poverty in the United States.
    New York, New York, Macmillan, 1962.

Hart, John F.   "Negro Migration in the United States," Annals of the
    Association of American Geographers, XLVIII (1958), p. 268.

Hathaway, Dale E.   "Migration From Agriculture: The Historical
    Record and Its Meaning," American Economic Review, L (May, 1960),
    pp. 379-391.

Herskowitz, Melville J.   The Myth of the Negro Past.   New York, New
    York, Harper and Brothers, 1941; Boston, Massachusetts, Beacon
    Press, 1958.

Hill, Joseph A.   "Recent Northward Migration of the Negro," Monthly
    Labor Review, XVIII (March, 1924), pp. 1-14.

Hines, Joseph. "The Functions of Racial Conflict," Social Forces, XLV (September 1966), pp. 1-10.

Hittell, Theordore H. History of California. 4 vols. San Francisco, California, N.J. Stone and Company, 1897, Vol. IV, 858 pp.

Holsey, Albon. "What is Negro Progress?" Opportunity, IX (January, 1931), p. 16.

Hunt, Rockwell D. and Nellie Van De Grift Sanchez. A Short History of California. New York, Thomas Y. Crowell Co., 1929.

Index to Selected Negro Periodicals Received in the Hallie Q. Brown Library. Vols. I-II. Wilberforce, Ohio, College of Education and Industrial Arts, Wilberforce University, 1950-1951.

Industrial Conflict and Race Conflict: Parallels Between the 1930's And the 1960's. Detroit, Industrial Relations Research Association, 1967.

Institute of Industrial Relations, University of California, Los Angeles, "Hard-Core Poverty and Unemployment in Los Angeles" (Washington, D.C., 1965), pp. 127-131.

International Index to Periodicals. Vols. III-XV. New York, New York, H.W. Wilson Company, 1920-1960.

Janow, Seymour J. and William Gilmartin. "Labor and Agricultural Migration to California, 1936-1940," Monthly Labor Review, LIII (July, 1941), pp. 18-34.

Johnson, Charles S. Growing Up in the Black Belt. Washington, D.C., American Council on Education, 19 41.

_____. Into the Main Stream: A Survey of Best Practice in Race Relations in the South. Chapel Hill, North Carolina, University of North Carolina Press, 1947.

_____. The Negro War Worker in San Francisco. San Francisco, California, 1944.

_____. Patterns of Negro Segregation. New York, New York, Harper and Brothers, 1943.

_____. Shadow of the Plantation. Chicago, Illinois, University of Chicago Press, 1934.

Johnson, Charles S., Edwin R. Embree and W.W. Alexander. The Collapse of Cotton Tenancy. Chapel Hill, North Carolina, The University of North Carolina Press, 1935.

Johnson, Charles S. The Negro in American Civilization. New York, New York, Henry Holt and Company, 1930, 538 pp.

Jones, Sam H. and James Ashwell. "Five Million Negroes Move North," Liberty (December 15, 1945), pp. 19-21, 73.

Josephson, Eric and Mary Josephson (eds.). Man Alone. New York, New York, Dell Publishing Company, 1965.

Journal of Negro Education. Vols. VI-XXI. Washington, D.C., College of Education, Howard University, 1937-1952.

Kennedy, Louise V. The Negro Pesant Turns Cityward. New York, New York, Columbia University Press, 1930.

Key, V.O., Jr. Southern Politics. New York, New York, Vintage Books, 1949.

Kolko, Gabriel. Wealth and Power in America, An Analysis of Social Class and Income Distribution. New York, New York, Frederick A. Praeger, 1962.

Consideration and Reference Tables prepared under direction of Simmon Kuznets and Dorothy Swaine Thomas, Philadelphia, Pennsylvania, American Philosophical Society, 1957.

"Labor in California and Pacific Northwest," Monthly Labor Review, LXIV (April, 1947), pp. 561-695.

Lacy, Virginia Mae. "United States Government Publications on the American Negro, 1916-1937." Unpublished Master's thesis, University of Illinois, 1938.

Landecker, Werner S. "Stratification in Urban Society." Principles of Sociology, Ronald Freedman et al. New York, New York, Henry Holt and Company, 1952, pp. 449-488.

Lasseter, D.B. "The Impact of the War on the South and Implications for Postwar Developments," Social Forces, XXIII (October, 1944), pp. 20-26.

Leggett, John C. Class, Race and Labor. New York, New York, Oxford University Press, 1971.

Lee, Everett S., et al. Population Redistribution and Economic Growth, United States, 1870-1950. Vol. I.

Lipset, Seymour M. and Hans Zetterberg. "Social Mobility in Industrial Societies," Social Mobility in Industrial Society, Seymour Lipset and Reinhard Bendix, eds., Berkeley and Los Angeles, University of California Press, 1959.

Logan, Rayford W. The Negro In American Life and Thought: The Nadir, 1877-1901. New York, New York, Dial Press, 1954.

Long, Norman H. and Charles S. Johnson. People vs. Property: Race Restrictive Covenants in Housing. Nashville. Tennessee, Fisk University Press, 1947.

Los Angeles County, The Annals of the American Academy of Political and Social Science, CCXLVIII (November, 1946), pp. 220-225.

Maclachlan, John M. and Joe S. Floyd, Jr. This Changing South. Gainesville, Florida, University of Florida Press, 1956.

Mangum, Charles S., Jr. The Legal Status of the Negro. Chapel Hill, North Carolina, The University of North Carolina Press, 1940.

Marshall, Albert P. "A Guide to Negro Periodical Literature," Vols. I-II. n.p., 1941-1942.

McCone, Violence in the City - An End or a Beginning? (Los Angeles, 1965).

McEntire, Davis. The Population of California. San Francisco, California, Parker Printing Company, 1946.

McGovney, D.O. "Racial Residential Segregation by State Court Enforcement of Restrictive Agreements, Covenants, or Conditions in Deeds is Unconstitutional," California Law Review, XXXIII (March, 1945), pp. 5-39.

McGraw, B.I. "Wartime Employment, Migration, and Housing of Negroes in the United States," Midwest Journal, I (Winter, 1948; Summer, 1949), pp. 20-29, 95-100.

McGroarty, John Steven. Los Angeles From the Mountains to the Sea. 3 Vols. Chicago: The American Historical Society. 1921, Vol. 1.

McWilliams, Carey. "Los Angeles: An Emerging Pattern," Common Ground, IX (Spring, 1949), pp. 3-10.

_____. The Great Exception. New York, New York, Current Books, 1949.

_____. *Factories in the Field: The Story of Migratory Farm Labor in California*. Boston, Massachusetts, Little, Brown and Company, 1939.

_____. *Southern California Country*. New York, New York, Duell, Sloan and Pearce, 1946.

_____. "The Los Angeles Archipelago." *Science and Society*, X (Winter, 1946), pp. 41-53.

_____. "They Still Keep Coming," New Masses, XLII (March, 1942), pp. 10-12.

Meier and Rudwick. *The Making of Black America* (New York, New York, 1969), Vols. I & II.

Meister, Richard J. (ed.). *The Black Ghetto*. Lexington, Massachusetts, D.C. Heath and Company, 1972.

Miller, Herbert A. *Races, Nations, and Classes*. Philadelphia, Pennsylvania, J.P. Lippincott and Company, 1924, 196 pp.

Miller, Loren, "Relationship of Racial Residential Segregation to Los Angeles Riots," MCA, X.

Mitchell, Broadus. *Depression Decade: From New Era Through New Deal*. Vol. IX of the Economic History of the United States. Edited by Henry David, *et al*. New York, New York, Rinehart and Company, Inc., 1947.

Moon, Henry Lee. *Balance of Power: The Negro Vote*. Garden City: Doubleday and Company, 1949.

Mowrer, Ernest Russell. *The Family: Its Organization and Disorganization*. Chicago, Illinois, The University of Chicago Press, 1932.

Myrdal, Gunnar. *An American Dilemma: The Negro Problems and Modern Democracy*. 2 Vols. New York, New York, Harper and Brothers, 1944.

National Negro Congress, Los Angeles Council. *Jim Crow in National Defense*, Los Angeles, 1940.

National Urban League. *Selected Bibliography on the Negro*. 4th edition. New York, New York, National Urban League, 1951.

"The Negro Moves West," *Fortnight*, XVII (October 6, 1954), pp. 23-26.

"Negroes in the California Agricultural Labor Force." Paper read at the 1958 meeting of the American Sociological Society, Seattle,

Washington, August, 1958.

Nelli, Humbert S. Italians in Chicago, 1880-1930. New York, New York, Oxford University Press, 1970.

Newmark, Harris. Sixty Years in Southern California, 1853-1913. New York, New York, The Knickerbocker Press, 1916.

Newmark, Maurice and Marco Newmark, Census of the City and County of Los Angeles for the Year 1850. Los Angeles, California, The Times Mirror Press, 1929.

"New Tithing Plan Aimed at Housing," New York Times, February 21, 1965, Section 8, p. 1.

Northrup, Herbert R. Organized Labor and the Negro. New York, New York, Harper and Brothers, 1944.

Oberschall, Anthony. "The Los Angeles Riot," Social Problems, XV (Winter 1968), pp. 297-310.

Osofsky, Gilbert. Harlem: The Making of a Ghetto, Negro New New York, 1890-1930. (New York, 1966)

Park, Robert E., Ernest W. Burgess and Roderick D. McKenzie, The City. Chicago, Illinois, the University of Chicago Press, 1925, 239 pp.

Parker, Michael. "Watts: The Liberal Response," New Politics, (Summer, 1965) pp. 41-49.

Powdermaker, Hortense, "The Channeling of Negro Aggression by the Cultural Process," American Journal of Sociology, May 1943, pp. 750-758.

Raine, Walter J. "The Perception of Police Brutality in South Central Los Angeles Following the Revolt of 1965," (1966), from an unpublished paper written for the U.S. Office of Economic Opportunity.

Ransford, Edward H. "Isolation, Powerlessness, and Violence: A Study of Attitudes and Participation in the Watts Riot," The American Journal of Sociology.

Raper, Arthur F. and Ira De A. Reid. Sharecroppers All. Chapel Hill, North Carolina, University of North Carolina Press, 1941.

Rause, James W. and Nathaniel S. Keith. No Slums in Ten Years: A Workable Program for Urban Renewal, Report to the Commissioners of the District of Columbia, January, 1955.

Reed, Bernice Anita. "Accommodation Between White and Negro Employees in a West Coast Aircraft Industry, 1942-1944," Social Forces, XXVI (October, 1947), pp. 76-84.

"Regional Differences in Jobs, Incomes, and Migration, 1929-1949," Monthly Labor Review, LXXI (October, 1950), pp. 433-437.

Reid, Ira De A. "Problems of Negro Migration During the War," Milbank Memorial Fund Quarterly, XXV (July, 1947), pp. 284-292.

Reimers, David M. (ed.). The Black Man in America. New York, New York: Thomas Y. Crowell Company, 1970.

Richardson, James F. The American City. Waltham, Massachusetts, Xerox College Publishing, 1972.

Rischin, Moses. The Promised City. (Cambridge, Massachusetts, 1962).

Rose, Harold M. The Black Ghetto. New York, New York: McGraw-Hill Book Company, 1971.

Rosenberg, Morris. "Perceptual Obstacles to Class Consciousness," Social Forces, 32 (October 1953), pp. 22-27.

Ross, Frank Alexander and Louise V. Kennedy. A Bibliography of Negro Migration. New York, New York: Columbia University Press, 1934.

Rowell, Edward J. "Drought Refugee and Labor Migration to California in 1936," Monthly Labor Review, XLIII (December, 1936), pp. 1355-1363.

Rudwick, Elliott M. Race Riot at East St. Louis, July 2, 1917. Carbondale, Illinois, Southern Illinois University Press, 1964.

Saloutos, Theodore. Farmer Movements in the South, 1865-1933 (University of California Publications in History, Vol. LXIV.) Berkeley, California: University of California Press, 1960.

Savage, W. Sherman. "The Negro in the Westward Movement," Journal of Negro History, XXV (October, 1940) pp. 531-539.

Schmidt, Ronald Ray, "Responses of Non-Negro Renters and Owners in Los Angeles and Orange Counties to the Prospect of Ethnic Change." Unpublished dissertation for the University of Southern California, 1965.

Schulman, Jay, "Ghetto Residence, Political Alienation, and Riot Orientation," in Urban Disorders, Violence, and Urban Victimization. Beverly Hills, California, 1968, p. 32.

Scott, Emmett J. Negro Migration During the War. New York, New York: Oxford University Press, 1920.

Sherman, Richard B. (ed.). The Negro and the City. Englewood Cliffs, New Jersey: Prentice-Hall, Inc., 1970.

Silberman, Charles E. "The City and the Negro," Fortune, March 1962, p. 89.

Sears, David O. "Riot Activity and Evaluation: An Overview of the Negro Survey" (1966), 1-2; an unpublished paper written for the U.S. Office of Economic Opportunity.

Silver, Allan, "The Demand for Order in Civil Society: A Review of Some Themes in the History of Urban Crime, Police and Riot," The Police, ed. David Bordua.

Smith, T. Lynn. "Characteristics of Migrants," Southwestern Social Science Quarterly, XXI (March, 1941), pp. 335-350.

Spaulding, Charles B. "Housing Problems of Minority Groups in Los Angeles."

Spear, Allen H. Black Chicago: The Making of a Negro Ghetto, 1890-1920. Chicago, Illinois, University of Chicago Press, 1967.

Sterner, Richard S. The Negro's Share: A Study of Income, Consumption, Housing, and Public Assistance. New York, New York: Harper and Brothers, 1943.

Storing, Herbert J. (ed.). What Country Have I? New York, New York: St. Martin's Press, 1970.

Street, James H. The New Revolution in the Cotton Economy: Mechanization and its Consequences. Chapel Hill, North Carolina: The University of North Carolina Press, 1957.

Swann, W.F.G., Walter Wheeler Cook, Charles A. Beard, John Maurice Clark, Karl N. Llewellyn, Madison Bentley, Arthur M. Schlesinger, William F. Ogburn, William I. Thomas, Essays on Research in the Social Sciences. Port Washington, New York: Kennikat Press, Inc., 1968.

Taeuber, Karl E. Negro Residential Segregation, 1940-1960: Changing Trends in the Large Cities of the United States, paper delivered

at the annual meeting of the American Sociological Association,
Washington, D.C., August 31, 1962 (Chicago: Population Research
and Training Center, 1963), pp. 5-6.

Taeuber, Karl E. and Alma F. Taeuber. _Negroes in Cities_. Atheneum,
New York: Aldine Publishing Company, 1972.

_____. _Negroes in Cities: Residential Segregation and Neighbor-hood Change_ (Chicago, 1965).

Tatum, Elbert Lee. _The Changed Political Thought of the Negro, 1915-1940_. New York, New York: Exposition Press, 1951.

Taylor, Paul S. and Edward J. Rowell. "Refugee Labor Migration to
California, 1937," _Monthly Labor Review_, XLVII (August, 1938),
pp. 240-250.

Taylor, Paul S. and Tom Vasey. "Drought Refugee and Labor Migration
to California in 1925," _Monthly Labor Review_, XLII (February,
1936), pp. 312-318.

Thompson, Warren S. _Growth and Changes in California's Population_.
Los Angeles, California, Haynes Foundation, 1955.

"Unemployment in 15 Metropolitan Areas," _Monthly Labor Review_,
January, 1968, pp. 5-6.

University of California at Los Angeles, Institute for Social Science
Research. "Social Science Research in the Los Angeles Area,"
Los Angeles, 1936.

University of California, Bureau of Public Administration. "Transients
and Migrants." Unpublished report prepared by Victor Jones.
Berkeley, 1939.

Wakstein, Allen M. (ed.). _The Urbanization of America_. Boston,
Massachusetts, Houghton Mifflin Company, 1970.

Warner, Sam Bass, Jr., _The Urban Wilderness_. New York, New York:
Harper and Row, Publishers, 1972.

Waskow, _From Race Riot to Sit-In_. Chapter 3. Garden City, Doubleday,
1966.

Weaver, Robert C. _Dilemmas of Urban America_. New York, New York:
Atheneum, 1969.

_____. _The Urban Complex_. Garden City, New York, Doubleday and
Company, Inc., 1966.

_____. _The Negro Ghetto_. New York, New York: Russell & Russell, 1948.

Wharton, Vernon Lane. _The Negro in Mississippi 1865-1890_. New York, New York: Harper & Row, Publishers, 1965.

Williams, Chancellor. _The Destruction of Black Civilization_. Dubuque, Iowa: Kendall/Hunt Publishing Company, 1971.

Williams, Dorothy Slade, "Ecology of Negro Communities in Los Angeles County: 1940-1959." (Unpublished dissertation for the University of Southern California, 1961.)

Williams, Walter. "Cleveland's Crisis Ghetto," _Trans-Action,_ IV (September 1967), pp. 33-42.

"Willie Stokes at the Golden Gate," _Crisis_, LVI (June, 1949), pp. 175-179, 187-188.

Wilson, James Q. _Negro Politics_, Glencoe: The Free Press, 1960.

Wilson, James Q., "Urban Renewal Does Not Always Renew," _Harvard Today_, January 1965, pp. 2-3.

Wirth, Louis. _The Ghetto_. Chicago, Illinois, University of Chicago Press, 1928.

Woodson, Carter G. _A Century of Negro Migration_. Washington, D.C., The Association for the Study of Negro Life and History, 1918.

Zawdski, B. and P.F. Larzarsfeld. "The Psychological Consequences of Unemployment," _Journal of Social Psychology_, 6 (1935), pp. 224-251.

U.S. GOVERNMENT PUBLICATIONS:

Annual Report of the Department of Health of the City of Los Angeles, California, 1931-1932.

Annual Report of the Los Angeles County Probation Department, 1932.

California State Chamber of Commerce. _Migrants: A National Problem and Its Impact on California_. Report and Recommendations of the Statewide Committee on the Migrant Problem. San Francisco: California State Chamber of Commerce, 1940.

Campbell, Angus and Howard Schuman, "Racial Attitudes in Fifteen American Cities," _Supplemental Studies for the National Advisory Commission on Civil Disorders_ (Washington, D.C. 1969).

Chicago Commission on Race Relations. _The Negro in Chicago: A Study_
of Race Relations and a Race Riot. Chicago, Illinois, University
of Chicago Press, 1922.

"1965 Crime Rate per 1,000 Population by District," a table compiled
by the Chicago Police Department.

Constitution of the State of California.

Dymally, Mervyn M. "Statement Prepared for the Governor's Commission
on the Los Angeles Riots," October 11, 1965.

Guide to the Records in the National Archives. Washington, D.C.,
U.S. Government Printing Office, 1948.

John F. Kraft, Inc., "Attitudes of Negroes in Various Cities (1967)",
pp. 4-7; a report prepared for the U.S. Senate Subcommittee on
Executive Reorganization.

Lively, C.E. and Conrad Taeuber. _Rural Migration in the United States_.
Works Progress Administration, Division of Research, Research
Monograph XIX. Washington, D.C., U.S. Government Printing Office,
1937.

McDowell, Afue, attorney, _Case No. 11838_. Supreme Court of the State
of California.

Post-War Housing, Report to the Senate Special Committee on Post-War
Economic Policy and Planning, by the Sub-Committee on Housing and
Urban Redevelopment, 79th Congress, 1st Session, August 1, 1945,
p. 17.

Report of the National Advisory Commission on Civil Disorders,
Washington, D.C., 1968.

State Relief Administration of California. "Migratory Labor in
California." Unpublished study prepared by the Division of
Special Surveys and Studies. San Francisco, 1936.

State Relief Administration of California. "Transients in California."
Unpublished study prepared by the Division of Special Surveys
and Studies. n.p., 1936.

_____. "Persons in Parties in Need of Manual Employment Entering
Arizona and California by Motor Vehicle, January 1 to September
30, 1942." Report No. 11. n.p., 1942.

_____. "Expenditures for Public Education in Los Angeles County
X: Total Current Expenditures, 1927-28 to 1936-37." Educational

Survey Bulletin No. 21. Los Angeles, 1938.

_____. "Expenditures for Public Education in Los Angeles County
    XII: Total School District Expenditures, 1927-28 to 1936-37."
    Educational Survey Bulletin No. 23. Los Angeles, 1938.

_____. "Summary Report of Skilled and White Collar Negro Survey
    Los Angeles County, 1935-36." Los Angeles, n.d.

_____. "The Story of the Negro in Los Angeles County, Prepared
    by the Federal Writers' Project." n.p., 1936.

U.S. Bureau of the Census, Current Population Reports, Series P-23,
    No. 17, "Special Census Survey of the South and East Los Angeles
    Areas: November 1965." Washington, D.C., 1966, p. 13.

U.S. Bureau of the Census, U.S. Censuses of Population and Housing:
    1960. Census Tracts, Washington, D.C., 1962.

_____. "The 1960's Riots: Interpretations and Recommendations"
    (1966), a report prepared for the President's Commission on Law
    Enforcement and Administration of Justice.

United States Commission on Civil Rights, "Location of Riots";
    Assistant United States Attorneys Reports. Chicago, Illinois,
    August 5, 1966; New York, New York, August 19, 1966.

U.S. Department of Labor. Publications of the Department of Labor.
    Washington, D.C., U.S. Government Printing Office, 1948.

Violence in the City - An End or a Beginning? (A Report of the
    California Governor's Commission on the Los Angeles Riots, 1965.)

Webb, John Nye. The Transient Unemployed. Works Progress Administra-
    tion Research Monograph III. Washington, D.C., U.S. Government
    Printing Office, 1935.

_____, and Malcolm Brown. Migrant Families. Works Progress
    Administration Research Monograph XVIII. Washington, D.C.
    U.S. Government Printing Office, 1938.

Results of Attempts to Contact Individuals for Research

Agencies and Professionals Contacted	Numbers of Referrals Given by Agencies and Professionals	Total Number of Referrals Successfully Interviewed	Number of Individuals Consenting To First Interview	Number of Individuals Willing to Participate In the Study	Research Individuals Fitting Criteria and Used in the Study
4 City Councilmen	31	2	11	10	5
8 Social Workers	40	31	17	14	11
13 Clergymen	45	35	34	30	27
7 Teachers	14	8	5	5	5
3 Probation Officials	None	None	None	None	None
2 Housing Officials	43	33	30	21	16
1 City Human Relations Office	10	8	8	8	7
3 Doctors	None	None	None	None	None
3 Attorneys	10	5	3	3	3
1 Dentists	None	None	None	None	None
5 Barbers	26	23	22	22	21
1 Elks Lodge	None	None	None	None	None
3 High Schools	35	33	30	30	30
1 NAACP	62	56	51	49	48
2 Newspapers	36	6	3	3	3
2 Funeral Homes	10	6	3	3	3
1 Urban League	44	41	31	29	29
1 Realtors	10	6	6	5	4
1 Policemen	None	None	None	None	None
2 Colleges	29	26	20	17	13
1 Black VFW	23	22	20	17	13
2 Trade Schools	20	16	14	13	11

67 Total

APPENDIX 2

Employment and Education Profile of Research
Participants by Sex and Age

Profession	MALE			FEMALE		
	Number Employed	Avg. No. of yrs. in School*	Average+ Age	Average Age	Number Enrolled	Avg. No. of yrs. in School
SKILLED PROFESSIONAL EMPLOYEES: (Lawyer, Doctor, Accountant, Teacher)	5	15	41	39	12	17
SKILLED EMPLOYEES: (Insurance Salesman, realtors, Gov't employees, soldiers)	35	8	48	44	45	11
SEMI-SKILLED EMPLOYEES: (office clerk, cook, auto mechanic, independent employment)	55	6	37	33	51	7
UNSKILLED EMPLOYEES: (janitor, domestic, garbage collector)	30	4	39	37	42	5
TOTAL	125	33	165	153	150	40

* High School Plus College; +Age at time of arrival in Watts

110

APPENDIX 3

I

INFORMAL ORAL INTERVIEWS

1. Where were you born?_____ Where did you live before you came to Los Angeles?_____ How long did you live there?_____ Parents?_____ God-parents?_____

2. How old were you when you came to Los Angeles?_____

3. Why _did_ you come to Los Angeles when you did? Explain.
_____
_____

4. Where did you reside?_____How Long?_____

5. How (by what means of transport) did you come?_____ How many came with you?_____

6. What did you do when you first arrived (in terms of occupation)? Describe. How long did you keep your first job?_____ Did you change jobs often?_____ How often?_____ About how long did you hold each job?_____

7. How did you find a place to live?_____

8. How many lived in your dwelling (rooming-boarding)?_____ How many were members of your (immediate) family? (Such as daughter, son, father)_____

9. How many people worked (approximately) at your company or place of employment?_____ In your crew?_____ How many black? _____ How many white?_____ Name of Company:_____

10. Did you work usually days or nights?_____ Did any of your close friends or family members work at the same place?_____
_____

11. Did you get paid by the day, week, every two weeks or monthly?
_____

12. Did your amount of money vary or did you receive the same amount?
_____

13. Did you belong to a union?_____ If yes, which?_____
    _____

14. Did you have to take an examination (any kind) in order to get
    your job?_____ How did you get your job? Apply outright,
    through a friend, or how?_____

15. Were there any whites working with you, or were you segregated?
    _____ How long did you work there?_____

16. Did or do you belong to a church?_____ Name of church?
    _____
    What kind of church activities were you involved with?_____
    _____ What responsibilities or jobs did you have
    in the church?_____ Parents?_____ Spouse?_____
    Kids?_____

17. Did you belong to any other kind of organization - social/civic,
    Elks, clubs, NAACP, Civil Rights groups?_____
    _____

18. What was the highest year of school you completed?_____
    Where?_____ How about your spouse (wife or husband)?
    _____

19. Were you satisfied with your job?_____ How about your pay?
    _____

20. Did you rent or buy a home between 1940-1946?_____ If so,
    where?_____ Did you ever try to move out?_____
    Were you satisfied where you lived?_____ (Overcrowded or
    what?)_____

21. Did you own a car then?_____ How did you travel to and from
    work?_____ Did most of your close friends own or have cars?
    _____

22. What was your opinion of the Police Department (i.e., the police
    officers)?_____ Were they Black?_____
    Did they live in the same neighborhood?_____

23. How (describe) were you treated by others (both blacks and whites
    with whom you came in contact)?_____

INFORMAL ORAL INTERVIEWS

1. From where did you come (state)?_____

2. Why did you come to Los Angeles?_____

3. What did you do when you first arrived?_____

4. What kind of work did you do?_____
   How Long?_____

5. How did you get to and from work?_____

6. How did you obtain your job? (Through a friend? Employment
   agency?_____ How?_____

7. How long did you work there?_____ Were you paid hourly,
   daily, weekly, monthly?_____

8. When did you come?_____ How many came with you?_____

9. How did you get here (car, train, what)?_____

10. Did you know anyone here before you came to Los Angeles?_____

11. Where did you live?_____ How did you find a place to live?
    _____

12. Did you rent a room?_____ A house?_____ What?_____

13. Did you eventually <u>buy</u> or own a house?_____ Did you own a
    car?_____ How about any member of your family?_____
    Your friends?_____

14. Describe the "physical area" where you lived ("run-down," "good
    condition," what)?_____ Were you satisfied?_____

15. How much schooling did you have before you came to Los Angeles?
    _____

16. Did you ever go back to school?_____ Did you attend voluntar-
    ily or because you had a chance to advance in your job status?____

17. How many were in your immediate family?_____

18. Did your spouse work too?_____ How about children?_____
    Who took care of them?_____ Did they attend schools?_____

Did they complete high school?_____ College?_____

19. What was your reaction/attitude toward other Blacks living in the neighborhood?_____

20. Why did Watts deteriorate in your opinion (jobs, no upkeep in housing, poor sanitation)?_____ Racial prejudice?
    _____

21. Did you want to move out of Watts?_____ When?_____
    Why?_____
    Did you eventually move - and if so, where?_____
    Was it, too, a Black or integrated neighborhood at first? Describe.
    _____

INFORMAL ORAL INTERVIEWS

1. The participants interviewed by the author came from the following states:

Alabama	34
Arkansas	17
Illinois	7
Kansas	10
Louisiana	70
Mississippi	36
Oklahoma	19
Texas	82

Responses

2. Why did you come to Los Angeles?

A.	Employment	203
B.	Climatic Conditions	17
C.	Relations or Friends	51
D.	No Response	0
E.	Other Response	4

3. What did you do when you first arrived?

A.	Contacted Relatives or Friends	21
B.	Sought Place to Live	210
C.	Sought Employment	40
D.	No Response	0
E.	Other Response	4

4a. What Type of work did you do?

A.	Defense Plant Labor	173
B.	Military Service	32
C.	Domestic or Janitorial Work	62
D.	Clerical Work (Small Business)	8
E.	No Response	0
F.	Other Response	0

4b. How long were you so employed?

A.	Less than 6 Months	7
B.	6 - 12 Months	58
C.	24 - 36 Months	201
D.	36 - 48 Months	5

```
        E.   Longer than 48 Months                          4
        F.   No Response                                     0

  5.   How did you obtain your job?

        A.   Through a Friend or Relative                  182
        B.   Newspaper (Want Ads)                           33
        C.   Employment Agency                              51
        D.   No Response                                     0
        E.   Other Response                                  9

  6.   How did you get to and from work?

        A.   Public Transportation (Red Car)              201
        B.   Automobile                                    60
        C.   No Response                                     0
        D.   Other Response                                14

  7.   How were you paid?

        A.   Bi-weekly                                    165
        B.   Daily                                         27
        C.   Weekly                                        41
        D.   Monthly                                       39
        E.   No Response                                     0
        F.   Other Response                                 3

 8a.   When did you arrive in Los Angeles?

        A.   1935 - 1940                                    43
        B.   1940 - 1945                                   101
        C.   1945 - 1950                                   112
        D.   Other Response                                19

 8b.   How many came with you?

        A.   Immediate Family (1 - 5)                      123
        B.   More than 5                                   117
        C.   No Response                                     0
        D.   Other Response                                35

  9.   How did you make the trip?

        A.   Train
             1.  Hitchhiking                                92
             2.  Regular (paying) Passenger                72
        B.   Automobile                                    97
        C.   Bus                                          103
        D.   Other Response                                11
```

10. Did you know anyone there before you came to
    Los Angeles?

    A. Yes   48
    B. No   227
    C. No Response   0

11a. Where did you live?

    A. Watts   213
    B. South Central Avenue   20
    C. West Adams Boulevard   21
    D. South Avalon Boulevard   11
    E. No Response   0
    F. Other Response   10

11b. How did you find a place to live?

    A. Friend or Relative Referral   259
    B. Newspaper Ads   11
    C. Realtor   5
    D. No Response   0
    E. Other Response   10

12. Type of Housing?

    A. Own a Home   53
    B. Rent/Lease   161
    C. Garage   56
    D. No Response   0
    E. Other Response   5

13a. Did you eventually buy a house?

    A. Yes   34
    B. No   241
    C. No Response   0

13b. Did you own a car?

    A. Yes   51
    B. No   211
    C. No Response   13
    D. Other Response   0

13c. Did any member of your family or friends own a home
     or car?

    A. Yes   55

B.	No	220
C.	No Response	0
D.	Other Response	0

14a. Were you satisfied with the "physical area" where you lived?

A.	Yes	25
B.	No	240
C.	No Response	0
D.	Other Response	10

14b. Was the physical area in satisfactory or unsatis-factory condition?

A.	Satisfactory	13
B.	Unsatisfactory	247
C.	No Response	2
D.	Other Response	13

15. How much education did you receive prior to arrival in Los Angeles?

A.	Grade School Only		197
B.	Junior High School		55
C.	High School		
	1.	Partially Completed	11
	2.	Graduated	4
D.	College		
	1.	Partially Completed	1
	2.	Graduated	0
E.	No Response		7
F.	Other Response		0

16. Did you ever go back to school?

A.	Yes		
	1.	Voluntarily	
	2.	Advancement Purposes	53
B.	No		171
C.	No Response		10
D.	Other Response		41

17. How many were in your immediate family?

A.	2 - 5	57
B.	5 - 10	148
C.	More than 10	61
D.	No Response	9

18a. Did your spouse work?

    A. Yes   241

A.	Yes	241
B.	No	24
C.	No Response	10

18b. Did your children work?

A.	Yes	89
B.	No	186

18c. Who cared for the children?

A.	Mother	19
B.	Father	21
C.	Older Brother or Sister	91
D.	Grandparent	49
E.	Aunt or Uncle	75
F.	No Response	9
G.	Other Response	11

19. What was your reaction or attitude toward other Blacks living in the neighborhood?

A.	Good to Excellent	19
B.	Fair to Good	20
C.	Poor to Bad	10
D.	No Response	40
E.	Other Response	186

20. Why did Watts deteriorate in your opinion?

A.	Poor Housing (Upkeep)	98
B.	Lack of Jobs/High Unemployment	151
C.	Racial Prejudice	3
D.	Poor Public Sanitation	22
E.	Overcrowding	76
F.	High Crime Rate	21
G.	No Response	0
H.	Other Response	4

21a. Did you want to move out of Watts?

A.	Yes	250
B.	No	25

21b. Did you eventually move?

A.	Yes	26

B.　No   249

21c.　If so, did you move to a Black or racially
      integrated neighborhood?

      A.　Black Neighborhood   251
      B.　Integrated Neighborhood   3
      C.　No Response   0
      D.　Other Response   21

OTHER TITLES AVAILABLE FROM
CENTURY TWENTY ONE PUBLISHING

Anderson, E. Frederick
   *The Development of Leadership and Organization Building
   in the Black Community of Los Angeles From 1900 Through
   World War II.* 1980. Perfect Bound. $12.00.
   LC# 79-93305. I.S.B.N. 0-86548-000-1.

Bonnett, Aubrey W.
   *Group Identification Among Negroes: An Examination of
   the Soul Concept in the United States of America.* 1980.
   Perfect Bound. $9.00. LC# 79-93304.
   I.S.B.N. 0-86548-001-X.

Butler, John S.
   Inequality in the Military: The Black Experience.
   1980. Perfect Bound. $10.00. LC# 79-65253.
   I.S.B.N. 0-86548-002-8.

Cogdell, Roy and Wilson, Sybil
   Black Communication in White Society. 1980. Perfect
   Bound. $13.00. LC# 79-93302. I.S.B.N. 0-86548-004-4.

Collins, Keith E.
   *Black Los Angeles: The Maturing of the Ghetto, 1940-
   1950.* 1980. Perfect Bound. $11.00. LC# 79-65254.
   I.S.B.N. 0-86548-005-2.

Dawkins, Marvin P.
   *Alcohol and the Black Community: Exploratory Studies of
   Selected Issues.* 1980. Perfect Bound. $9.00.
   LC# 79-93301. I.S.B.N. 0-86548-006-0.

Ellis, Arthur L.
   The Black Power Brokers. 1980. Perfect Bound. $12.00.
   LC# 79-65252. I.S.B.N. 0-86548-009-5.

Fujita, Kuniko
   *Black Worker's Struggles in Detroit's Auto Industry,
   1935-1975.* 1980. Perfect Bound. $10.00. LC# 79-93300.
   I.S.B.N. 0-86548-010-9.

Jones, Marcus E.
   *Black Migration in the United States with Emphasis on
   Selected Central Cities.* 1980. Perfect Bound. $11.00.
   LC# 79-93299. I.S.B.N. 0-86548-014-1.